IN DEFENCE
OF THE SOUL

KEITH WARD

ONEWORLD

OXFORD

IN DEFENCE OF THE SOUL

Oneworld Publications
(Sales and Editorial)
185 Banbury Road
Oxford OX2 7AR
England

Oneworld Publications
(US Marketing Office)
PO Box 830, 21 Broadway
Rockport, MA 01966
USA

ISBN 1–85168–040–3

Cover design and illustration by Design Deluxe
Printed and bound in Finland by WSOY

CONTENTS

INTRODUCTION

THIS IS A BOOK ABOUT THE SOUL. It is about human dignity, value and freedom. It is about the unique and irreplaceable worth of every human life. And it is about the strange and startling fact that there are many strands of modern thought, propagated with the deepest sincerity and seriousness, which threaten to undermine and destroy all these considerations. Even the word 'soul' is scarcely used any more, and few could say just what it means, or what the idea of the soul really is. There are many who think that science has shown that human beings are basically just like other animals; that they are products of random mutations and impersonal cosmic processes; that they are purely material organisms, destined to die and rot like flowers or weeds. It is rare to find humans regarded as souls created by God for an eternal destiny, and with an awesome moral responsibility for their own lives. For has science not shown that the human species is just a tiny and unimportant part of a vast material cosmos, without purpose, value or meaning?

It is undoubtedly true that there has been a revolution in our way of thinking about the universe in the past three hundred years. In that very short space of time, the amazing progress of the physical sciences has led us to a quite new appreciation of human life and its place in nature. Things can never be the same again. We cannot, and should not, turn our backs on the scientific revolution, which has shown us truths beyond the comprehension of previous generations. The sciences of physics, astronomy, geology and biology, in particular, have led us to see human existence in a vast cosmic perspective of mathematically elegant law and evolutionary development, hardly guessed at before the seventeenth century.

But when the sciences begin to touch on the nature of humanity, on what it is to be a human being, then they may seem to have implications of the most far-reaching importance. Writers who have popularized science have not been slow to point out these implications. Richard Dawkins, Jacques Monod, Desmond Morris and many others have all written popular and influential books, proclaiming that science has now entered the secret citadel of the human soul, and found it empty. Human persons, they say, are not free spiritual agents with a special dignity. They are physical organisms for reproducing genes; and, as such, they have no more intrinsic dignity than walking bags of chemical compounds. All they have is an absurdly inflated sense of their own significance, which science is now in a position to deflate very rapidly. For such writers, talk of the soul can be no more than a relic of superstition, a tinge of sentimentality for our own species, without any basis in fact.

So we come to stand at a sort of crossroads, one that may seem rather theoretical, but is of absolutely decisive importance for our own future. What is at stake is our whole view of what it is to be human; whether we can really continue to believe in human dignity and value; whether all traditional moral values must not collapse in the cold clear light of scientific truth. Those who wish to continue to think of the soul are concerned to protect the inherent preciousness of human life, its sacredness and possession of particular rights and obligations. Those who reject all such talk will see humans as objects for scientific manipulation; and the world they will come to inhabit, if it continues to exist at all, will be a world beyond morality, dignity and freedom; a world of the manipulation of truth, of morality and of ideology, in the name of whatever powers come to replace the God whom science has killed.

I do not think this overstates the situation we are now in. Though the decline of morality and religion that marks western culture may be thought to be a localized phenomenon of cultural tiredness, its roots are in fact deeper and more universal. For the decline is occasioned by the clear-headed insight that human life does not have purpose or dignity; and that is said to be produced by rational, scientific investigation. Thus the choice is between rationality — which undermines moral and religious conviction — and the resurgence of the irrational, in a desperate and panic-stricken flight from science into astrology, or occultism or some long-outmoded legendary or fantastic cult of the irrational. This choice is clear in contemporary western societies, where institutional religion is weakened and divided by self-doubt and uncertainty, and where astrology and the occult are eagerly studied by readers of popular newspapers and fiction. But every culture in our world faces, or will have to face, the same battle between the science that undermines moral commitment and the superstition that places it beyond rational justification or criticism. The choice between cynicism and fanaticism is an uncomfortable one, but it seems to be the one there is.

This book is written in the belief that this is indeed the apparent choice we are faced with, but that in fact it has been subtly misstated. Something has gone terribly wrong, and it is, basically, that the popularizers of science have misconceived both the nature and proper limits of scientific truth. It is they, and not the religious, who are the dogmatists and high priests of orthodoxy now. A careful and accurate view of scientific theories and discoveries will show that, though dramatic, they do not at all undermine belief in the human soul, its distinctiveness and unique value. Indeed, in a deep and convincing way, they strongly reinforce it, because scientific activity itself, in its dispassionate quest for rationality and truth, shows a commitment to certain absolute moral values and the transcendence of the human spirit over its own material environment. So what I have done is try to trace some of the major influences that have led to the highly persuasive but subtly misconceived attack on the reality of the human soul. I begin with Nietzsche (chapter 1), whose famous proclamation of the 'death of God' became a sort of declaration of war on the reality of a spiritual realm. Like many who followed him, however, Nietzsche continued to insist on the worth of human freedom, not seeing that once the attack on spirit has begun, it must be followed through until it has been driven from its last refuge in the human skull.

I trace the development of that attack in the work of many biologists who claim support, rightly or not, in the pioneering work of Darwin, for their view that purpose can play no part in human evolution (chapters 2 and 3). I look at the work of Freud and some psychoanalysts, who reduce the importance of consciousness in human life, and who attack conscience-morality as a dangerous and possibly pathological feature of human psychology (chapter 4). And I consider the work of Marx, the basic and explicit materialism of which undermines all claims to human individuality and uniqueness in any significant sense (chapter 5).

What I have tried to do is to show how the attack on the soul has developed with seeming inevitability, until religion and morality themselves come to seem strange curiosities, pathologies of the human mind. And I show how many contemporary philosophers contribute to this development, by failing to provide any convincing basis for moral commitment or for the respect for personhood they usually espouse (chapter 6). The morality of liberal rationalism thus comes to be seen as an insecurely based prejudice in favour of certain likes or interests, deprived of power to move the will.

The culmination of the attack comes in the work of neurophysiologists, geneticists and computer technologists, who often assume as obvious the view that all human experiences are caused solely by brain-states that are fully explicable by laws of physics (chapter 7). So they complete the quest for total manipulation of human consciousness, and the reduction of persons to the status of laboratory artifacts. The process that began with the rejection of God and developed by the rejection of objective morality culminates in the denial of human dignity, and in the paradox that the resolute pursuit of reason seems to lead to the triumph of the irrational, for what reason in the end exposes is its own non-rational foundations.

Throughout the text, I have tried to disentangle the valuable truths that have been discovered by proper scientific investigation from the many half-truths and misconceptions that have fuelled the attack on the soul. Along with many particular criticisms, I have singled out one view as especially important and especially unjustifiable. It is what might be called the world-view of scientific objectivism – the view that the analytical and reductionist techniques of the most successful experimental sciences provide the whole truth about every aspect of the real world, in a value-free and completely objective, impersonal way. In the final chapter (chapter 8), I develop a positive view of scientific activity as a deeply moral commitment to reason and truth, which must accept that its techniques are only applicable to certain aspects of the world (broadly, the exactly measurable, general, law-like, closed and controlled system aspects), and are thus by definition bound to be partial and abstract. A proper understanding of science, such as is now increasingly held by physicists, in particular, does not undermine belief in the soul at all. On the contrary, it increases our sense of reverence, as we contemplate the unique transcendence of a being which, while part of nature, can understand and comprehend its own reality.

We are all now faced with the questions, 'Is there such a thing as the human soul? Does it make sense to continue to think that human beings are morally quite special? Is there anything decisively and definitively important about human life, that we should respect it?' We all have to answer these questions for ourselves. I hope that what I have written will expose the central arguments that have led to an attack on the idea of the soul and show how weak they really are. I hope that we may then be able to see what it means to say that the soul exists and to see the importance of affirming it. We might also be able to see the great importance of objective morality and of belief in a supreme value and goal of human endeavour not, as Nietzsche thought, as threats to human freedom, but on the contrary as the only defence of human value and dignity in a world in which they are increasingly under threat.

1

THE GOSPEL OF
FALSE FREEDOM

'GOD IS DEAD', wrote the philosopher Friedrich Nietzsche in 1882.[1] He saw this as a great liberation for humanity. God was, after all, a great omnipotent being from whom there could be no escape; who was always watching to see what you did, prying and condemning. He was the great tyrant, and we had to obey Him in fear and trembling, or He would consign us to everlasting hell-fire. For centuries, this God had kept human beings in servile fear; and the discovery that He did not exist was like discovering real freedom for the first time. If there is no God, then there is no superior being to tell you what to do or to punish you for not doing it. There is no infallible oracle to take all decisions out of your hands. There is no repressive and absolute power, from which there is no escape. For the first time, human beings are free – free to be themselves, to make their own decisions, to live their own lives and pursue purposes and goals that they construct for themselves.

This is, for Nietzsche, a sort of gospel, a 'good news' that liberates one from a life of spiritual bondage into true human maturity. It is the gospel of the modern age, of man who has achieved technical mastery over nature, and who can fashion it to his own purposes. It is impossible to understand twentieth century western culture without feeling something of the idea of freedom and self-mastery that this gospel preaches. Nietzsche died just as the twentieth century was dawning. He did not live to see the spread of this gospel throughout the whole world. Whether he would have approved of its effects is impossible to say. But, even before his death, there were signs that this gospel was not all that it claimed to be. Friedrich Nietzsche himself became insane; perhaps it was no mere co-incidence that the modern apostle of human freedom did not achieve spiritual liberation and human fulfilment. Instead, he found mental disintegration and despair. Such despair was the true heritage of his gospel to the world.

Despair is the consequence of this gospel of freedom, because in the end such freedom is empty. It leaves you alone in the world, free to do anything in a world in which nothing is any longer worth doing. Our freedom, our power over nature, is indeed enormous – vastly greater than Nietzsche himself could have suspected. We have arrived at a quite new situation in the history of the earth. We have got to the point where we can actually begin to control our own natures, through genetic engineering, as well as the world around us. For the first time in history, we have the power to destroy the whole earth, through nuclear holocaust. We can drastically alter the whole nature of our environment, through the use of chemical products. It seems that we have a potentially limitless power over ourselves and our world; we have ourselves become gods, creators of life and death.

We human beings are the creators now. We have the power to create the world in our own image. Yet, with all this power and freedom, we remain young, inexperienced, rash and greedy, able to control the world but unable to control our own desires. When there was a God, He set the limits of life and death. He gave us a set of moral rules to live by. He gave us a purpose to pursue and bound us to obey His commands. But now, if God is dead, there are no limits except the ones we ourselves invent. Our power is unchecked by anything other than our own autonomous decisions. And the question is, can we cope with such power? Are we really ready to take the future of our world and our species completely into our own hands?

If you are an incorrigible optimist, you might say yes. But a sober look at human nature suggests that, for all our intelligence, we are still basically animals, driven by lust and rage, fear and envy. Morality – those commands that God lays down for human life – was a check on these instincts. Even if it was an infantile check, or some sort of social illusion, at least it worked to some extent. However much hypocrisy and cruelty there has been in Christian culture, at least lip-service has been paid to a set of moral rules and principles – principles of justice, honesty and loyalty. This has set limits on the open exercise of power and forced people to restrict their desires to some extent, where they threatened to harm others. People have been expected at least to pretend that they are good; and that appearance has saved civilization from disaster and collapse.

However, if it comes to be clearly seen that morality is an illusion, which can and should now be dispensed with, we will come to chaos. Our intelligence has taken us beyond morality, and we will do whatever we can, merely because it is possible – even to the point of self-destruction. The strange and terrible thing about modern man is that our greatest gift, the ability to pursue knowledge and truth, seems to have become our greatest enemy. For, if Nietzsche is right, it leads us to overthrow the old religious and moral standards and limitations, and offers nothing to put in their place. Where everything is permitted, everything will be done; the powers of chaos and destruction will be unleashed in open conflict upon the world. And that is just what Nietzsche frighteningly preached – the rule of the 'Superman', the man beyond morality, who will impose his will by force upon the cowering herd. 'I teach you the Superman', he said, 'Man is something to be surpassed.'[2]

The immediate response of humanist thinkers is to say – well, if this is the way it is, we must keep morality, and perhaps religion too, just for its usefulness, even if it is not really true.

'If there were not a God,' Voltaire wrote, 'it would be necessary to invent him'[3] – to keep the masses in order. But, of course, we cannot keep religion and morality for their usefulness, when they are clearly known not to be justifiable. They retain what power they have only when we believe that they are valuable for their own sake alone. We cannot persuade ourselves to believe something just because it might be useful – not, at least, if we are reasonable at all. And if we tried to impose such beliefs on others, our whole society would have to be founded on deceit – which would undermine the very morality we were trying to encourage in others. If we have to face up to the fact that God is dead, and morality is finished, we will have to accept the consequences. But at least we can see that this gospel of freedom is not quite as liberating as it might have seemed. If what it threatens to bring is chaos and destruction, we may wonder whether we should accept it quite so eagerly. Perhaps there is more to be said for God after all.

I most definitely do not want to suggest that we ought to believe in God because it will be safer or because it will make us happier or because it will prevent chaos. It is never a good justification for believing something that it will cheer us up or make us feel happy. Sooner or later, we will have to ask, 'But is it true?' And if it is not, we will simply have to give the belief up. It may make me happy to think that I will never fall ill or die but that is not a good reason for believing it. Whether or not it makes me happy, the question of truth must come first; it cannot be ignored. So what we have to ask is whether it is *true* that there is a God who created us and who desires our good. Many objections to belief in God, however, have not been attacks on its truth, but have held that such belief is somehow objectionable or even immoral. Thus Nietzsche and many other modern philosophers – Jean-Paul Sartre in France, Patrick Nowell-Smith in England – have attacked the idea of God, and of religious morality, not because it is false, but because it is infantile or morally objectionable.[4] The basic argument is that if being moral is a matter of obeying the commands of an all-powerful being, that is just unquestioning obedience. It is infantile and does not really have any moral value at all. The real moral values are those of freedom and self-determination; and they can only exist if there is no God. That is the argument I want to look at first. It is a very widespread one; so much so, that you can often find it taken for granted that religious morality must be oppressive and reactionary, or that belief in human freedom or autonomy is a distinctively modern idea, which springs from the rejection of God. I am sure that both these beliefs are quite mistaken, and could not be historically justified. But I am also sure, as I have implied, that the allegedly modern doctrine of human freedom is not a life-enhancing liberation at all. On the contrary, it is a doctrine which, when its full implications are seen and explored, is destructive of all that is important and distinctive about human life and culture. The gospel of freedom from God is in fact a gospel of slavery to passion. So I want to attack this gospel and expose the mistakes upon which it rests.

But of course it has not come to exert the huge power over modern minds that it has, without some reason. Although it is perverse and mistaken, it has been a reaction against a way of putting religious positions that was itself dangerously inadequate and one-sided. Modern atheism is the judgement of God upon modern religion. Religious institutions have sometimes been oppressive and reactionary; forms of belief have been intransigent and ossified; religious life has been a matter of conformity and gloom, rather than of life and joy. This modern gospel has perceived something that the ancient gospel of Christianity has sometimes lost sight of. So, in looking at it rather critically, we should try to bring out those positive aspects that can only gain their true meaning within the context of religious faith. Freedom and maturity are religious concerns, too, but sometimes it takes an atheist to remind us when we are in danger of losing them. That job has been done. It is now time for theists to remind the modern atheists of the vast and irreplaceable treasures they will lose if they fail to see that God shows us what true human freedom is in the great revealed traditions of religion.

Though all religions have much of vital importance to say about morality, Nietzsche's attack was specifically upon Christianity, and it is a Christian view that I will now attempt to defend. But virtually everything in this defence will be appropriate to other religious faiths, as they seek to respond to the attacks of European secularism in their own way. What, then, is the Christian view of morality, and why have atheists objected to it so much? It is undoubtedly true that the Christian view of morality derives, in the first place, from the Old Testament Law, called, in Hebrew, the 'Torah'. In the Sermon on the Mount (Matt. 5–7), Jesus teaches that the Law is revealed by God, and that it was not simply to be abandoned by His disciples, but to be deepened and enriched (Matt. 5:17–19). The written Torah consists of everything from Genesis 1 to the last chapter of Deuteronomy, everything in the first five books of the Bible. The Ten Commandments are only a very small part of the Torah, even though they are very important. According to Jewish tradition, there are 613 commandments in the Torah, and Jesus taught (according to Matthew's gospel) that even the least important of these was to be obeyed 'until all things were fulfilled'. These laws cover many very different things, from not eating pigs or rabbits to loving your neighbour as yourself. They include matters such as circumcision, rules for religious feasts and for the treatment of various skin diseases. They are not all what we would call 'moral rules', in the present sense of the words. But, according to the tradition, they are all rules given by God to Moses in the wilderness; and they are all to be obeyed by the people of Israel.

The first and most obvious fact about this Torah is that morality cannot be separated from belief in God. There are no neat distinctions between personal morality, politics and religion. The laws cover all these things; they are rules given by God to set apart this people, in the whole of their life, for His service. Morality is not thought of as a set of conventions that people make up to govern their relationships with one another. All the basic rules for human conduct are God-given, and so they have absolute authority. Of course, Christians see most of these laws as embodied in the person of Christ, rather than as written down as a set of rules for society to follow – the laws about sacrifices, for example, are no longer binding, because Christ has fulfilled for ever all that sacrifice was meant to do, as the letter to the Hebrews asserts. But Christians share with Jews and with Muslims the basic under-standing of morality as something not man-made, but God-given. It is a set of commands from the Creator Himself, and so has an authority and force that is absolute. For Christians, these commands are to be interpreted in the light of the life and teachings of Jesus, but that life and teaching are absolutely definitive for Christians. A Christian cannot separate out a man-made, conventional morality from an authoritative Divine revelation. All his morality is given by Divine authority.

At once, the defender of human autonomy will leap to the attack. First of all he will object to seeing morality as a matter of commands. He does not, of course, think that there is a God to command anything, so he has to believe that all moral rules are made up by human beings. But he will also object to the idea of God dictating 613 rules, which Moses merely had to write down passively, and which the Israelites had to obey, even if they could not see the point of them. Isn't there any place for thought and decision-making in morality?

Now it is a total misunderstanding of the Divine Law to think that it is just a set of written rules, which cover every human situation, which people just have to apply without thinking. There are numerous principles, but they need to be very carefully interpreted, and that takes a great deal of thought. No Jew or Christian with any sense wants to take a law in the Bible, just as it stands, and apply it directly to a quite different situation today. We do not, for example, stone people to death any more, even though many Old Testament rules mention stoning to death as a penalty. What we need to do with the biblical laws is much more complicated. We need to look at them in their original context (laws about the conquest of Canaan, for example, cannot be applied to the modern world). We need to try to find the underlying principles they express. We need to get all the relevant facts of the modern situation. We need, if we are Christians, to interpret all the laws in the light of the example and teaching of Christ. And we need to seek the guidance of God in seeing how these principles are to be applied to our own case. All this takes a very great deal of thought, of practical wisdom and of prayerful reflection. Christians do not think that they have the answers to all moral problems ready-made in the Bible. Like anybody else, we need to think and reflect and decide, often with great difficulty. And the same goes for the Jewish use of the Torah and the Muslim use of the Shari'a, the Koranic law, too.

But the difference is, that we are not free to think and decide anything we want. Even though there are not detailed answers in the Bible, there are principles and insights there which are binding on us. It is rather like the way in which a judge might appeal to the law in England. There will be some precedents that he will look at. There may be some statutes to which he will have to conform. But at the end of the day, he has a case before him that is almost bound to be unique in some ways. So he not only has to apply a ready-made law; he has to develop it, and to use all his skill and training in doing so. So what the Christian has is a set of precedents and principles. He cannot move beyond these, but he still has to apply and develop them, when new cases come along.

God has given us the precedents for our moral thinking. He gave these in the Jewish Law. For Christians, the person of Jesus becomes a sort of living embodiment of the Law. He does not directly answer our modern moral problems. But reflection on His life, and prayerful fellowship with Him, gives us the basic perspectives on human life beyond which we must not go. He is our model of what is right. But this model does not restrict or stop our independent thinking. On the contrary, it inspires and guides it to deeper levels. So the first objection – that making morality depend on revealed commands must give rise to unquestioning obedience and lack of thought – is totally misplaced. We must obey God, of course. But that obedience is more like a life of discipleship than like following a rule-book. It takes thought and reflection and prayer. It is more like growing closer to someone we love than it is like blindly obeying some impersonal instruction manual. And there is nothing infantile or inhuman about that.

But now a second objection comes up. Surely obedience is not a virtue, but a vice? When we are mature, we have to make our own decisions and take responsibility for them. It is simply no defence to say, 'I was just doing what I was told'. Can't obedience be morally dangerous? After all, that's just what the Nazi war criminals said in their defence: 'We were only obeying orders.' And surely that just isn't good enough. Mustn't we throw out obedience, then, as a dangerous and undesirable thing?

The answer to that is, it all depends on what or whom you are obedient to. We couldn't have any sort of society where we were never obedient to anybody. Young children must obey their parents, because – we hope – the parents will want to protect them from harm, and will sometimes have to tell their children not to do certain things, even though the children are too young to see they are dangerous. If I say to a child, 'Don't go near the fire', I hope it will obey me, even if it doesn't know that it will get burned otherwise, and that is the reason I gave the order. In a similar way, we often have to obey what our superiors at work say, or what the government says. There would be total chaos if we did not accept that we had to do some things just because we were told to. We can't have everybody going around deciding what to do for himself – whether to go to work today, or what to do when we get there. If anything is going to get done, there has to be some obedience – doing what you are told by somebody who has the authority to tell you.

Now of course this obedience should not be unquestioning. When I was ordained, I swore an oath to obey my bishop 'in all things lawful'. So, if he tells me to go and kill one of my church-wardens, or to stop praying, I need not obey him; in fact, I definitely should not. This is because even bishops are human. They can make mistakes or even command things that are evil and unlawful. So we should not give unquestioning obedience to any human being. We should normally obey, but in the end we must be true to our own consciences, and refuse to do what we clearly see to be wrong.

Christians have always said this, anyway. Your own conscience comes first. Even though you might be mistaken, you must follow your own conscience; you must never do what you believe to be quite clearly wrong. That is why, at the Nuremberg war crimes tribunal, the defence that the Nazis were only obeying orders was not accepted. The prosecution argued that no rational person could have failed to see that they were being ordered to do something evil. So they should have refused to obey. Believers will certainly accept this argument. But it is not really relevant to God. God cannot make mistakes and He will never command us to do anything evil; so it is always right to obey God. Moreover, it is always reasonable to obey God, because He knows the conditions of human life and its dangers better than we do. He should – He made them.

The real trouble here is not with obeying God. It is with whether we can be sure that certain commands really come from God. I think we can be absolutely certain that it is right and proper to obey God and do whatever He tells us. But we cannot always be certain of what God is telling us. It is only too obvious that many people claim that God is telling them things, when He is not. If somebody said, 'God has just told me to kill my granny', we can be pretty sure that he is either lying or deluded. But how do we know when something *is* revealed by God?

There are three basic tests. One is that the revelation must be made on the authority of one who is an outstanding moral example, a person of wisdom and understanding, and one whose life shows a deep relationship with God in prayer. Only such a person can be a friend of God and thus a trustworthy source of revelation. Second, the revelation must provide an insight into a way of living that is truly fulfilling and effective. Revelation is not just the provision of facts about the world; it is a disclosure of the right way of living, the way to eternal relationship with God. So there must be a confirmation of its power in the lives of those who follow it, as they experience growing knowledge and love of the Divine. And third, if a revelation is from God it must show the power of God and be attested by those paranormal events that we call miracles, whether of healing, fulfilment of prophecy or gifts of deep understanding of people's problems. Only if these three tests are fulfilled should we seriously consider something to be a revelation. But in the end, God reveals Himself to whom He will, and our response will be a personal response to a challenge God puts to our hearts. Under these conditions we are justified in taking God's revelation as our ultimate authority. Our obedience still doesn't have to be unquestioning, of course. Because we still do need to work out exactly what that revelation is saying to us today, and it is possible for us to draw the wrong conclusions. All I am saying is that it is perfectly possible both to put conscience first – to say that I will never do what I clearly see to be wrong – and to obey the revelation of God. For He does not tell me to do what I see to be wrong. On the contrary, He expands and deepens my understanding of what is right, and of how I should be living.

This provides an answer to the questions, 'Why should God bother to tell us anything? Why can't I just work out what is right and wrong for myself?' On many matters, I can work out what is right and wrong for myself. It doesn't need God to tell me that murder is wrong; that stealing and lying are wrong; that exploitation and oppression are wrong. I know these things, from the perfectly simple fact that I wouldn't like any of them to be done to me, and that they are bad things to do to anybody who has feelings like mine. I may, of course, ignore other people's feelings or not care in the slightest about them. But at least we all know that, if we are impartial, it is wrong to do such things to people. Is God just reminding us of what we already know, then?

Not at all. Those rules, though they are very important, are just the basic minimum that is required in any human society. Human life is about more than keeping a few basic minimum rules. It is also about human flourishing and fulfilment, about the realization of a purpose and the attainment of an eternal destiny that consists in relationship with God. We can get hints of God's purpose in creation and of a human destiny both for this world and beyond death – no human culture is without some beliefs about these things. But it does need God to tell us what the true human purpose – the purpose He intends for humans – really is, and what our final destiny is, and how we can achieve it. He shows us what the perfectly fulfilled human life is like – and that may come as something of a surprise to those who think that human fulfilment is just a matter of more pleasure and self-satisfaction. God tells us that our real fulfilment lies in losing our selves, in caring much for the weak and the poor, and in caring little about wealth and possessions.[5] And God also tells us what our final destiny is – it is, in a way we could never have foretold or been sure of on our own, to be united with the life of God Himself in glory.

What God reveals and puts before us in His revelation is how we should be living, what our hopes should be centred on, and what we should be obedient to. We should be obedient to the living God, and that means we should be seeking to walk with Him in love. How can such obedience be dangerous or immature? If man is made for eternal fellowship with God, then for man to try to live alone, out of his own resources, out of relation to God, is a terrible weakness. Perhaps it is better to speak of 'fellowship' with God rather than obedience to God, if the word 'obedience' puts you off. But we need to remember that in that fellowship, between a very imperfect creature and the almighty creator of all things, it would be very odd indeed if we insisted on either dominating or in ignoring the wishes and purposes of God. I must confess that I cannot see much wrong in obeying the wishes of a perfectly good, wise and loving God, simply because we love Him and want to do what He wants.

However, I expect the objector will jump up again and say, 'But surely, if you have to obey God, you must be doing so out of fear of punishment? You are reducing morality to a sort of long-term prudence, or even a bit of reasonable self-interest. Is that what you really want?' Talk of prudence and self-interest, however, just seems to be missing the point completely. Undoubtedly, if we do not follow the principles God has laid down for his creation, we will suffer harm. We will in fact do ourselves terrible harm if we allow ourselves to become self-interested and callous and cruel. Religious believers do not really say that if you are cruel to somebody else, then God will in turn be cruel to you, by toasting you over a fire for ever. How could a God who is always proclaiming forgiveness and mercy ever do that? The religious insight is very much deeper. It is that if you are cruel to somebody else, you begin to turn yourself into the sort of person who cannot recognize kindness when you see it. You slowly become incapable of appreciating the feelings of others. You become incapable of love – you will not be able either to give it to somebody else or to receive it from them, either. Because, if you are going to accept love from others, you must at least respect them as persons, of value in their own right. And that is just what you have made yourself unable to do. You will only be able to regard others either as threats to your own selfish well-being or as objects for you to manipulate for the sake of your own pleasure. You will have forgotten what love is.

That is what hell really is. There are many images of hell in the New Testament. There is the image of the rubbish-heap outside Jerusalem (Gehenna); the image of being shut out of a great feast, lonely and unable to enter; and the image of outer darkness, where the soul is isolated, excluded from love.[6] The tragedy is that God is not doing the excluding. The soul itself is excluding itself from love, because it cannot recognize or accept love for what it is. God's love is still there – He is present in hell as well as everywhere else. But the soul will have made itself unable to accept it. We make hell for ourselves, as we daily forget or hide from ourselves what love really is.

The fear of hell is not just selfish fear of being hurt. Truly seen, it is the fear of becoming the sort of people who are unable to love, who exclude themselves from love. So the fear of hell is a perfectly good reason for obeying God. But a much better reason is the hope of heaven. And again, that is not a selfish hope for lots of goodies in the next life. Heaven is the presence of God. So the hope of heaven is the desire to be with God, in His presence, and to enjoy Him for ever. Now if somebody does not believe in God, he obviously cannot do what is right out of the fear of hell or the hope of heaven. He must do it for its own sake. There is nothing at all wrong with that. The believer also does what is right because it is right. But he has two extra very powerful motivations. He does not want to become the sort of person who is unable to give or receive love. And he wants to know and love God, the most perfect and glorious of beings, and so find what is of the very greatest value. He also wants to help achieve the purposes of this God, just because of his love and admiration, and his gratitude for all the good things God gives. Far from revealed religion undermining morality, then, it adds new and strong dimensions to morality. Morality is not reduced to prudence; it is enriched and expanded into love. We might well think that only in a spiritual context can morality be seen for what it truly is.

So we can see how very wide of the mark is the atheist's often-reiterated claim that religious morality is infantile; that it is just a matter of blind obedience to a tyrant God. The God of true religion, of Judaism, Islam and Christianity and of many Indian devotional traditions, is a God of mercy, of compassion and unlimited love. If He gives moral commands, it is in order to show us the way to eternal life, to our own true good, and to our fully personal maturity. Of course, if you take some of the Old Testament laws in isolation, they can seem rather pointless and outdated – nobody now wants to apply the laws in Leviticus about the treatment of spots. But it takes wilful blindness to find the essence of either Jewish or Christian morality there. Jesus summarized the matter supremely when

He pointed out the two greatest laws, in the light of which the others must be interpreted and applied to changing circumstances: 'You shall love the Lord your God with all your mind and heart and strength' and 'You shall love your neighbour as yourself'.[7] These are the basic elements of Christian morality. It is not just unlikely, it is completely impossible to obey these commands out of fear or blindly. Love requires sensitive understanding and sympathy; love drives out fear for ever; love is the fulfilling of the law.

I hope that we can now at least get the atheist to withdraw his charge that Christian morality, and theistic morality in general, is somehow infantile or objectionable. The believer is not going around trying to oppress everyone else by forcing his own moral beliefs on them. He is in fact trying to point out that morality is above all a matter of love and of forgiveness and compassion; and that, if people are to accept it, that must be because they perceive it to be the highest and most admirable claim on human life. But the believer can go on to point out that morality is, in the end, a claim on human life. It is not some sort of optional extra or something that we may decide freely to adopt. Any theory of human freedom which says that it is quite all right if we decide to kill or hate other people is perverse and depraved. And that is the trouble with Nietzsche, or at least with many of those who have adopted his teachings at face value.

The French philosopher and novelist Jean-Paul Sartre made the theme of human freedom one of his main concerns in many of his novels and plays. His main philosophical work, *Being and Nothingness*, contains a section at the end on what he calls 'moral seriousness'.[8] This is the belief that there are objective moral values that stand over against man, telling him what he must do and therefore limiting his freedom. Sartre always saw God, too, as standing over against man telling him what to do. So he thought that if there was a God, man could not truly be free. He would always be under the orders of this supreme being; he would have to conform to standards imposed on him from outside; he would be a slave, not a free man at all.

Sartre completely rejected moral seriousness. He completely rejected the thought that there was a real, objective God, or that there were objective moral values or rules. After all, if there is no God, where would these rules be? There is no heavenly rule book in which they are written down. And, in a materialist universe there is just no place for such odd things as objective moral values. The only alternative, Sartre thought when he wrote *Being and Nothingness*, was that there are really no moral values at all, unless we make them up ourselves. Values are just the projections of our own desires and decisions on to the external world. So we really are totally free, in the sense that we can make up our own moral values and principles; we can act in any way we choose, and there is no objective, non-human power to stop us (except the blind forces of nature, which we are free to overcome if we can).

Thus Sartre proclaimed a view of human life in which there are no objective moral claims or demands. There is complete freedom to do as you wish, and perhaps the most important thing is to escape from convention and live in the way you really want. This philosophy – it is perhaps the best-known form of the philosophy generally known as existentialism – was very influential. It inspired many young people, especially, who felt stifled by the conventions of their elders, and who now felt able to drop out of society and try to discover what they really wanted. Its strength lies in its protest against mere convention, against always being worried about what other people will think, about conformity. It must be said that Christianity has always protested about mere conformity, too. A faith founded on the life of a man who was killed as a non-conformist can hardly be one that thinks much of convention. Indeed, the angriest words of Jesus are directed precisely at the traditions of the scribes, who were worried about the observance of outward rules more than about real love and compassion. And in Judaism and Islam there can be no doubt that outward deeds performed without a true intention of the heart are vain.

But, if you get rid of convention and conformity, what do you put in its place? This is where the weakness of Sartre's position becomes apparent. For all he said was, 'There are no objective values, so you must just choose'. But there are two very powerful objections to this. First, what if I choose to kill or torture people? You might ask me to consider what I would feel like if I was in their shoes. But I might simply reply that I am not in their shoes, and the more pain they feel, the better I like it. Now if you think that's a terrible attitude to have, aren't you really saying that I *should* not think that way? That I am not really free, after all, to do whatever I choose. I *have* to take other people into account. And now we're back to objective moral values again. Other people place a claim on me; and if I don't see it, there is something wrong with me.

Sartre himself came to see this point. He later admitted that he could not just look at a starving child and say, 'I am free to kick it to death, if I choose'. No; if I really see that child and understand its pain, I am not free to ignore it. Or, at least, I am free to ignore it – no one will stop me doing so. But I am not *morally* free. There is a claim to care for other people, and Sartre came to admit that was true.[9]

The second main weakness of Sartre's early position is that there is simply no vision in it, when you examine it closely. At first, it looks exciting – free yourself from convention, it says, and live as you choose. But when you try it, you find that nothing is much worth choosing any more. Boredom begins to take over. The only answer to the question, 'What should I do?' is 'Whatever you want'. Things begin to lose their significance and importance. People need a vision. 'Without vision, the people perish'.[10] They need to believe that they are doing something worthwhile; that there is a goal to be achieved; and that it really is important, even if some other people would disagree. It isn't just a matter of you choosing to do something; it's more a matter of coming to see that something ought to be done, and that it's your job to do it.

Now Sartre came to see this, too. He saw the need for vision, for a worthwhile goal, for commitment to a significant task in life. What he did was to become a Marxist. Whatever we think of that, it does give a vision of a future goal to aim at. It is in many ways the very opposite of existentialism, which it sees as a rather woolly, liberal ideology. It does believe, in one sense, in objective moral values – values I do not merely choose myself, but which are somehow written into the nature of things. I will be examining Marxism later, and do not wish to criticize it now. My point is that Sartre himself perceived the weakness and danger of believing that morality is just a matter of decision and personal choice. What begins by looking like a noble appeal to human freedom and dignity is soon exposed as a view that actually undermines the importance and dignity of human life, by taking away all objective value and purpose from it.

The believer would say that we need freedom from mere convention; we need a vision that can inspire human idealism and heroic action. We need a sense of moral claim – not something repressive, but something exciting and challenging. A believer would go on to say that what makes human life important, what gives it dignity, is precisely the fact that we are free to accept or reject such moral claims. We are free and responsible; we can choose between right and wrong; and so we can decide our own eternal destiny. We come to a sense of our own humanity at times when we do sense a moral claim upon us. We feel that we will be betraying our own humanity if we do not respond by commitment. We come across a situation – it may be we happen to meet a handicapped child or a case of exploitation at work. And we feel, 'I just have to do something about this'. We can be cowards; we can turn aside. But if we do, we are less free and not more free; we make ourselves less human. We become more human the more we do respond to these moral claims and recognize them. For it is in freely responding to them that we grow in understanding, in sensitivity, in humanity.

What we experience, when we meet such a moral claim and recognize it for what it is, is God himself. An atheist is unable really to make any sense of talking of an 'objective moral claim'. Where would it be? What sort of thing is it? Whereas a theist can say that a moral claim is our sense of the presence of God, challenging us to action and response. It is the sense of an almighty and all-wise being, not compelling us to do something, but making it clearer to us what His purpose is, what love requires, what He urges us to do. It is this sort of experience that makes the difference between knowing what is right and wrong, in the abstract, and feeling the obligation to do what is right, feeling the personal demand made upon us now.

Whenever people slip into talking about morality in terms of 'demands', 'claims', 'requirements' or 'imperatives', they are testifying to a sense, however obscure, of the presence of God, and to His essential place in morality. Without God, this whole way of thinking about morality begins to crumble; and that is why religion is vitally important to morality after all. It is not that people cannot be morally good without believing in God or without being religious. Of course they can. Yet our whole understanding of morality really does depend upon the existence of God, upon seeing human conduct in the context of a wider spiritual reality, if it is to make sense. Christians put this by seeing in Jesus one who calls us, explicitly and unequivocally, to a life of total discipleship, to being perfect as God is perfect. He makes the demand underlying all morality quite open, and He shows that He Himself is its source. Followers of other traditions find, in a similar way, that their understanding of morality is changed radically by seeing it as a response to the self-disclosure of God, by which He shows a way to union with the Divine Being itself.

In this chapter I have spoken of Christianity because that is the religion Nietzsche attacked and because I belong to the Christian tradition. But I hope it will be readily seen that the arguments I have used can be used on behalf of all theistic faiths, so that it is the religious view of life that has been so travestied by Nietzsche that is the defence against the despair his philosophy can breed. It may be wondered how what I have said applies to the non-theistic traditions of Indian religion, and especially to Buddhism, which is often called atheistic. It is obvious that Buddhism does not lead to the consequences I have been warning against, yet it does not believe in God, and would perhaps share with Nietzsche some misgivings about the authoritarian and infantile nature of much theistic religion. How can this be?

Buddhism is indeed a special case, and in this book I am really talking about the contribution that theistic religions can make to correcting the western moral malaise. Yet I would be sorry to think that Buddhism was wholly ignored, so perhaps one or two suggestions may be helpful. The Buddha does not teach the existence of a creator God who is the source of a revealed moral law, with whom we are to attain fellowship by faithful obedience. Nor does He speak of the existence of 'the soul', as a substantial core of human personality. Yet the Buddhist way is a pursuit of a state of supreme objective value – called *nirvana* – which can be attained, and was attained by Gautama. Though that state is not fully describable, it is one of supreme bliss and knowledge; and it is from the Buddha's supreme knowledge that He teaches the way to the spiritual goal and release from suffering for all. So there is a supreme goal; it is not just invented by us; and it can only be achieved by intense moral striving and mental discipline. While there are no revealed commands of God, there is the *dharma*, the law of right living and thinking, which is written into the structure of the universe. While there is no personal relationship with God, there is a realization of a supreme reality of knowledge and bliss, in which we find completion and rest. While there is no immaterial soul, created by God, it is certainly true that humans are not simply material organisms.

For Buddhists, the soul consists of bundles of qualities, and there is no one enduring self that ties them together. Buddhists do not believe in a soul, as one continuing subject of experience and action. Yet they do believe that human beings are free to do good or evil, and that their decisions will have vital consequences for the future. So there is complete agreement with theistic traditions that human persons have value and dignity, are responsible for their own future existences and should aim at the supreme goal of enlightenment. They can achieve that goal ultimately by following the teaching of the Enlightened One, who gives them the laws leading to their final good. In this way, Buddhism shares with other faiths the central concern I am describing, a concern to affirm the existence of the spiritual nature of humanity and the existence of a goal of supreme value. That is what, as a theist, I am calling the existence of the soul and of God, who is both the goal and the origin of human life for theists. So when I say that our view of morality depends on affirming the existence of God, that must be seen in the context of theism, the context in which the attacks on religion in the West naturally originated. But I hope it is clear that I also mean to say that our view of morality depends on affirming the existence of a supreme objective value, as more than subjective or based on personal inclination. That is what a global view of religion can give, and what is so much needed as a response to the subjectivism and materialism of our age.

I began with the gospel of Nietzsche, promising human liberation, freedom from God and His demands, from morality and its repressive force. I have tried to suggest that this gospel is a sham, and that what it really provides is despair and a great trivializing of human effort and dignity. It was trying to stress the need for true human freedom and escape from the tyranny of opinion or convention. But it entirely failed to see that these are the concerns of real faith in God, too. It entirely failed to see the importance of morality in human life, and the very basic connection between morality and belief in God. I have been mostly concerned to show that religious morality is not the negative, authoritarian thing it was accused of being. And I have also tried to show how religion and morality are connected more closely than some people think.

But human dignity and uniqueness have been attacked from other sides, too. Indeed, our age has seen an attack on the human soul of such magnitude that it threatens to eradicate the idea completely. Nietzsche's mistake was to think that human self-mastery could only be achieved if religious ideas were finally given up. But at least he was still concerned about human self-mastery and freedom, about human uniqueness and dignity. The next strand of modern thought I shall deal with is one that directly attacks the idea of human uniqueness and freedom, that proposes a view of humanity as no more than a biological organism. If it can make its case, the whole idea of a soul created by God, or, in the broader interpretation, of a spiritual being with a final goal of supreme objective value, and with the unique freedom to know and choose between good and evil, disappears. So it is vitally important to examine and assess the arguments in this area, and see just how strong they really are. The arguments do not come from experimental biology itself, but from popularizers of science, who are using some of the findings of biological science to make broader generalizations about human nature as a whole. It is the strength and status of those generalizations that we must examine.

2

THE ELIMINATION
OF PURPOSE
FROM THE UNIVERSE

AT ABOUT THE MIDDLE of the nineteenth century, biology underwent a major intellectual revolution. Until that time, it had been dominated by Platonic or Aristotelian ideas, according to which living things fell into very clearly demarcated species or natural kinds. These species were fixed and changeless; and the boundaries between them were decisive and clear. There was a common belief that living things were distinguished from non-living things by the possession of a 'life force' or 'living soul' or principle of activity. This life force was an extra factor, distinct from purely physical forces, and it accounted for the special properties of living things – their properties of self-organization and reproduction.

All these ideas began to be undermined in the nineteenth century, and biology is still today making discoveries and working on assumptions that challenge or overthrow them. The first ideas to go were that biological species were changeless and rigidly distinct from each other. The key figure in bringing about this change of view was, of course, Charles Darwin, with his theory of the development of species through natural selection. There had been thinkers before that time who had suggested that living organisms had evolved from simpler forms of life. The philosopher Immanuel Kant published a work in 1755 which asserted that all living organisms had evolved from inorganic matter in accordance with mechanical principles.[1] But Darwin was one of the first to cast such a theory in a truly scientific form, in which it could explain a vast amount of zoological and archaeological data, and could even be experimentally tested in some specific cases.[2]

The traditional view had been that God created each species directly. This was true both in classical Greek thought and in the biblical tradition, which at least seemed to imply that God made each species fully formed and was opposed to blurring the boundaries between them. Some of the Old Testament laws forbid mixing dissimilar things (like linen and wool); and it may seem that this is based on a view that different types of thing cannot or should not mix. In the case of man, it was often held that God supernaturally inserted a soul into the animal form, so that man was absolutely different in type from the other species. Thomas Aquinas, writing in about 1266, taught that what we call 'the soul' is the life-principle, the 'form' or distinctive character of living things. All organisms have souls. These souls are not substantial; they do not exist apart from the body. They are rather principles of nutrition and movement, which make living things distinct from non-living things.

Animals, he believed, have 'sensitive souls', which give their bodies the powers of knowledge and sense-perception. These 'sensitive souls' come into being by natural processes of nature; they cannot exist without the bodies they inhabit or inform, and they die when their bodies die. All these beliefs derived from the *De Anima*, a work of the Greek philosopher Aristotle. But then Aquinas introduced a quite new element. He held that, in human beings, there is a different sort of soul, a rational soul, which no other species possesses. 'Man', he wrote, 'is non-material in respect of his intellectual power because the power of understanding is not the power of an organ.'[3] By 'understanding', Aquinas meant the power of rational thought, of comprehending the natures of things, of forming general concepts, discerning logical relationships and thinking intelligently. This activity, he held, could only be performed by something incorporeal – non-bodily. Furthermore, it would be substantive, or capable of existing on its own. And it would be incorruptible, since, not being material, it cannot decay or dissolve into smaller parts, as bodies do at death. So the rational soul of man cannot originate by natural processes from matter. It must be directly created by God. And it does not die when the body dies, but goes on existing for ever – unless God Himself destroys it.

This human or rational soul is thus completely different in kind from anything else in nature. It is substantive, spiritual and immortal, directly created by God. Nevertheless, the soul on its own is not complete, because the soul is still basically 'what actuates a body of a certain kind'; that is, it is still essentially the form of a particular body. The human soul can exist on its own for ever, thinking and understanding. But it needs something to think about; and it needs some way of expressing its thoughts in action. In other words, it needs a body. The body provides the sense-perceptions, which are the material for thinking. And it provides a means of acting and relating to other things in the world. Without a body, there can be no sense-perceptions, no movement, no feelings and no real interactions with others. So Aquinas says that the soul 'has an essential and natural tendency to embodiment'. It is very important to see that, for him, souls are not just temporarily imprisoned in bodies. The human, rational soul performs the functions of the sensitive and the nutritive soul as well – there is only one soul in each person. But, even though it can exist on its own, it does so only in an unnatural and imperfect way, because its real job is to be the form, the living principle, of a particular body. What Aquinas was doing was to try to tread a middle way between Plato, who saw the body just as an unnecessary appendage to the soul; and Aristotle, who denied any immaterial, substantive soul at all. Aquinas wanted the human soul both to be capable of independent existence, and to be essentially the form of a particular body.

It is a consequence of all this that, though human souls exist after death, they do so in a very imperfect way. They are not really persons at all – they can only be persons when both soul and body are joined in a unique, distinctive way. They have no sense-images or sense-memories. All they can have is a purely intellectual understanding of things – and even then, in an 'unnatural, confused and general' way. Now this may not be quite as bad as it sounds – for even a confused knowledge of purely spiritual things, which God gives the soul directly, might be such a wonderful thing that we can scarcely imagine it. Still, it is not fully personal existence; and it is not really what Christians hope for. That is why Aquinas was perfectly happy with the Christian doctrine of the resurrection of the body. Only when we got our bodies back at the resurrection, he thought, would we be proper persons again. So resurrection becomes an essential part of his theory of the soul.

Now this was written 800 years ago, long before the biological sciences had achieved even their present state of knowledge. I doubt if anyone could today accept it just as it stands. Nevertheless, it is important to know what was actually said by the man who is perhaps the most important theologian in Christendom. Many of the ways we talk and think now derive, perhaps unknowingly, from what he said, or from slight distortions of what he said. We can see, in particular, how Aquinas was able to make a rigid and absolute distinction between man and the other animals, a distinction that we might not wish to make quite so absolute. In animals, the soul (the actuating principle of life) does provide sensations; but it is naturally generated and dies with the body. In man, the soul is directly inserted by God into a body that has been prepared for it. Of course, Aquinas had to face the question, 'When does this happen?' When is the soul created by God?

He did propose an answer to this question. His answer is that as the human embryo develops, it first of all has a sensitive or animal soul, naturally generated. Later on it comes to have a rational soul. But, since each man only has one soul, the sensitive soul has to be destroyed or dissolved by

God at the very moment when he inserts the rational soul into the body. This happens, says Aquinas, 'at the completion of man's coming into being', which he elsewhere conjectures happens after forty days for males and ninety days for females[4] (since, according to Aristotle, females were failed males, males who hadn't quite made the grade, and so were typically rounded and shapeless instead of well-formed and angular, like decent males). What happens at the early stages of embryonic development, then, is that matter is disposed to receive a certain kind of form. And when it has reached the proper stage of development, God pops the form in, to complete the process.

What happens, we may wonder, if God decides not to pop a rational soul into a suitably developed piece of matter? Aquinas, who was never reluctant to face hard questions, raises this question with regard to embryos conceived as a result of fornication. Shouldn't God simply refuse to create a soul that results from such an immoral act? he asks. But his reply is that, though God disapproves of the fornication, he approves of the creation of children, so he will create a proper soul, when the matter is ready for it.

As we consider this account with the hindsight of 800 years, two questions are almost bound to occur to us. First, can we really think of God as sitting around waiting for pieces of matter to be suitably formed, so that He directly creates a rational soul whenever the conditions are right? Surely the appeal to God's direct, indeed virtually miraculous, action is here superfluous. If the sensitive souls of animals can develop naturally, so can rational souls. Perhaps we can get at what Aquinas was trying to say by recalling that, for him, the point was that a spiritual soul cannot be caused just by material processes – the greater cannot come from the less. But the soul has to come from somewhere. So it must be directly created by God. The crunch question is this: can new and 'better' forms of life develop or emerge or evolve from lower forms of life? If they can, then we simply have no need of this doctrine of direct creation.

This leads straight on to the second question, which is: 'If the human embryo can naturally develop through various stages of life, why can species not develop in a similar way, so that new species emerge in the course of a continuous process of development?' Once that question has been posed, it seems quite possible that just such a thing has happened on this earth. And embryologists often point out that the human embryo does 'recapitulate', in a small way, the development of life on earth through greater and greater complexity until rational consciousness appears.

Now the revolutionary change that came over biology in the nineteenth century was precisely the recognition that life on earth had emerged from much simpler forms. New and different forms did come into existence; so the species was not fixed and immutable. Rather, there is a continuity in all life, so that one species can develop gradually into another, over millions of years. The idea of fixed and absolute boundaries between species disappeared, and the idea of 'emergence' became dominant. But is there anything anti-Christian or anti-religious in this? I cannot see why.

Jews, Christians and Muslims believe that God created the world out of nothing. If we say that complicated life-forms emerged from less complicated ones, and they ultimately emerged from nothing, all we are doing is inserting another step in the process of creation. There is simply no problem at all. If you are still tempted to say that 'the greater cannot come from the less', the decisive answer to that is – well, it can, if God makes it. The creation of the world out of nothing is the biggest and best example there could ever be of the greater coming from the less. Of course, things don't really come from absolutely nothing. There has to be a God, theists think, who brings them from nothing. But, if there is a God, He can bring better things out of worse things if He wants to. So the modern scientific world-view does accept that human life is part of a continuous and emergent process, created by God. There is nothing to worry believers about that in the smallest degree.

But that is not the end of the story. For Charles Darwin's theory, or at least the development of it in the light of more exact knowledge of genetics, has been so successful that the vast majority of biologists take it for granted now; and it suggests a mechanism of evolution that may worry believers. The developed theory states that living organisms are subject to random mutations. Most of them are harmful, of course, and those mutated individuals die out. But, over a long period of time, some of them prove to be better suited to survival in a largely hostile environment than others. Those mutations breed more successfully, and so tend to predominate. Such mutations go on happening, so that each species now on earth has originated by a long series of mutations from a distant, but probably common, set of sources – something like the one-cell amoeba – and the whole process has been an entirely non-purposive and non-directed one. It is quite accidental that well-adapted mutations continue to occur.

On this view, far from being a specially created and providentially endowed being, man is presented as a result of a multitude of random mutations, some of which happened to be best adapted to survive in their particular environments. There is no guarantee that this process of adaptation will continue. Man, as a species, may well die out or perhaps mutate into something quite different. There is nothing specially final or significant about the particular form of the human species. This seems a far cry from the biblical teaching that human beings are made in the image of God, and that their existence is in some way the final purpose of the whole universe.

The Christian clergy were quite right to be worried by this theory, even though a few of them rather made fools of themselves at the 1860 Oxford conference of the British Association at which Bishop Wilberforce tried to take on the scientific might of Darwin and Huxley, only to be deservedly ridiculed. The worry is not simply that man is descended from a monkey, as some less enlightened Christians put it. The worry is that it has all happened by chance. The fittest survive, but whether there will be any fit organisms at all, or what they will have to be like to survive, is an open question. For such a view, it seems quite impossible to believe that only the human species has a soul, or that it is the final goal of evolution.

It is in fact misleading to speak of Darwin's theory as a theory of 'evolution', for the word evolution does suggest progress or development, and thus a sort of purposiveness – as opposed to devolution, which implies decline or decay. But a biologist cannot regard the changes in organic matter on the surface of this planet as a development, or as a decline either. In so far as he is a scientist, he must merely record, in a neutral way, the changes that do take place and attempt to explain or predict them. It is better to think of the theory as one of mutatory survival or something similarly neutral and non-purposive. So it seems that if the theory is successful, it is directly incompatible with religious thinking about organic life, which speaks of it as a result of God's plan or purpose. It is equally incompatible with those Indian religious views that see the present material forms of human life as a result of a sort of ignorance – *avidya* – which is the result of selfish desire. For these views, too, any biological account that removes any moral purpose or causality from nature must be considered as deeply inadequate.

What is the believer, and especially the believing biologist, to say to all this? Well, it should first be noted that Darwin's theory is not quite the same sort of thing as a theory in physics. It does not state some general laws which certain entities always follow, so that, given their present state, their subsequent behaviour can be accurately predicted. What it does is to say that reproductive organisms mutate at random. Some mutations die out and others survive. They survive because they happen to be better adapted to their environment. And these facts alone are sufficient to account for the variety of animal species we now have. The theory does not enable us to predict either what mutations will take place in future, or which ones are likely to survive. Physical laws can be tested under laboratory conditions while 'laws of evolution' cannot.

So, to make its case, Darwin's theory has to establish that it is the only theory able to account for the variety of animal species, and that it is adequate to account for that variety. It is clearly very difficult to establish these claims; perhaps they could never be established with certainty. For there is only one example available to us of an evolutionary process; it cannot be compared with others to check the probability of it happening by pure chance. Of course, it is a simpler explanation than one appealing to design of any sort, but that does not show that it is really adequate, that no appeal to purpose is either necessary or possible.

In the first place, it is quite possible to accept Darwin's theory, and believe that the whole process that has culminated in man has been, and still is, guided by a purpose. After all, it is a process that started with the existence of some very simple organisms, relatively speaking, and a few general laws. Those organisms – things like viruses or amoebae – were of no great value in themselves, and were barely distinguishable from lumps of inorganic matter. Yet the process has developed so that it now contains whole communities of exceedingly complex beings, with central nervous systems and brains that can store information, have consciousness and purpose and thought, and can come to awareness of what they are and direct their own future. Through that process, inorganic, unconscious matter has become aware of its own nature and looks like becoming capable of consciously deciding on its own future. On any account, that fact is totally remarkable. It clearly *looks* as if there has been a purposive development towards self-consciousness, ability to master the environment, and complexity. It is almost impossible to resist the impression that this has been a supremely purposive process, developing from very simple forms towards states of greater consciousness, value and capacity.

If a biologist says that this process has come about by a whole host of random mutations and interactions with a wider environment, there is no need to deny that at all. It is rather like saying that my purposive movement from one place to another, in order to see the view, has come about by a whole host of muscular movements and bodily interactions with my environment. Of course it has; if it hadn't, we could never have learned how to move about at all. But if a biologist says that I need *only* talk about muscular movements, about physics and chemistry, and that will *completely* explain my movements, we would find that rather odd. The obvious explanation of my movement was that I wanted to get a better view. The biologist is not concerned about that. He does not mention it in his account, because he is not interested in it. But if I want an adequate explanation of my movement, I need to talk about that purpose as well as the chemistry of muscular movements. One does not conflict with the other. Both are there. The only conflict comes when the biologist says (if he is silly), 'I can explain this all in terms of muscle motions; so your whole movement was really non-purposive; purpose is a delusion'.

The fact is that talking about purpose and about the mechanism of my bodily movements is not a matter of two conflicting scientific theories. They are two different ways of talking about the same thing; and we need both of them for different purposes – one when we are doing biology, and one when we are wondering what to do next. Looked at properly, the religious view of man and Darwin's theory of natural selection can co-exist quite happily, as long as neither transgresses its proper limits. Theology should not make statements about scientific matters of fact that conflict with the evidence – such as that God created each species simultaneously, exactly as it now is. The Genesis story of Adam and Eve should not be read as a scientific and literal account, but as a pictorial and important statement about the distinctiveness of human life and its relation to God. But biological theories should not make statements about Divine creation or purpose that fall outside their proper scientific discipline. God could quite easily have so constructed the laws of the physical world that they would in due course, by the methods of natural selection, lead to the development of conscious rational beings like man. There is no need at all to talk about 'accidents' or about things happening quite by chance. Indeed, to talk in that way is to ignore the fact that to speak of processes as random is just another way of saying that we have no precise explanation for them. They may be too complicated, or it may seem more trouble than it is worth to explain them, or we may simply not know how to explain them fully. A random process is just one for which we can provide no complete explanation.

It might be said that a physicist with enough time and patience could provide exact predictions that would transform the fuzzy idea of randomness into the clear precision of necessity. That, however, is just what quantum physicists would generally now say is impossible in principle. In modern particle physics, it seems that some elements of indeterminacy are bound to remain, in any full account of the physical universe.[5] In other words, randomness, inexplicability, cannot be completely eliminated, according to the best contemporary scientific practitioners. Since randomness is only another name for ignorance, it may well be that some forms of purposive explanation in nature would be required for an adequate explanation of its processes.

This is not a forlorn request for a return to the discredited philosophy of 'vitalism'. Nor is it a rejection of the amazing success of analytical techniques in molecular biology. It is a statement of the simple fact that what a mechanistic scientist may call 'random' may in fact be 'purposive', or guided partly by final causation. Mechanistic techniques will never discover that, for they are not concerned with it. But they cannot reasonably deny it, for what must remain random to them may well carry the marks and impact of purpose, in the evolution of life in this universe. That is a hypothesis that cannot be established by the experimental techniques of biology. It must be assessed by a wider consideration of the relation of the processes of evolution to the emergence of worthwhile values. There are many biologists who do see evolution as seemingly directed to the emergence of more creative or valuable states. Thus Dobzhansky writes, 'Determinism . . . is becoming gradually relaxed as the evolution of life progresses. The elements of creativity are more perceptible in the evolution of higher than in that of lower organisms.'[6] That is, deterministic, mechanistic explanations alone do not give an adequate account, at least of the later stages of the evolution of life. Some biologists would go much further. Rupert Sheldrake thinks that we need to use concepts of purpose to interpret all biological phenomena;[7] and though his view is regarded by many biologists as rather extreme, it certainly cannot be held by any reputable scientist that the experimental findings of biology have either established a wholly deterministic account of evolution, or have strictly proved that the course of evolution is not purposively directed.

Like most of the natural sciences, the foundations of biology are not so secure now as they seemed a little while ago. But I do not want what I say to depend solely on this fact. I think that, whichever way that argument – about whether organic life needs non-mechanistic modes of explanation or not – goes, the believer in God is not in fact under threat.

If it turns out that the process of life can be fully explained in terms of a few basic physical and chemical laws and principles, the believer in God can point out that these laws were created by God, that God can tell exactly where they will lead, and thus He could easily have designed them to lead just where He wanted. It is rather like a computer programmer who inserts a program into his computer. Everything then proceeds by perfectly simple, mechanistic principles. Yet the whole process is purposive from start to finish, and it accomplishes exactly what the programmer intended – at least, if he was clever enough. (Naturally, this does not rule out the possibility of miracles, since God can amend the laws whenever He feels like it.)

If, on the other hand, it turns out that we do need to resort to other principles in biology to explain the facts fully; if we have to admit that there are features that mechanistic principles alone cannot explain; if our best attempts at explanation have to leave room for creative adaptations and new dynamic forces, which can better account for the seemingly ceaseless urge of natural life towards new and more complex forms, then the believer in God can point to God as the director of and continual influence on this dynamic process. Again the impression of conflict between biological process and purpose is dissolved when we look at it more carefully.

Now the views of modern biology do have an impact on theology. We cannot now believe that God created each species directly as it now is. And we cannot believe that God is constantly interrupting the processes of the natural world, to push things along by direct control, whenever they are in difficulty. There is a change of view here from Aquinas, for example, who thought that angels were constantly causing changes in the physical world, pushing the stars around their celestial spheres and so forth. We now see the physical universe much more as governed by its own internal laws, as not needing spiritual influences to keep it going. What we have to remember is that for the theist, God is the author of all those laws. Without Him, they would all collapse in a moment and cease entirely. Things in the universe do not keep going by some inherent power of their own. It is God who makes all things exist, and who ensures that they will keep acting in accordance with what we call the regular laws of nature.

Another very important thing to remember is what a tremendous dogma it is that events will go on obeying the 'laws of nature'; indeed, that these laws will apply always and everywhere, even to the furthest galaxies in space. It is an absolutely huge step of faith to believe that events will always behave in accordance with regular – and indeed mathematically beautiful – principles. If we look hard at the evidence for that faith, it seems to be something like this: things in our universe generally do act in predictable ways. Sometimes the unexpected happens, but we rather assume that there will be some sort of explanation for it. So it is a commonsense belief, when we think about it, that things normally behave in regular ways. But, as far as common sense goes, they need not always do so. And we may not know what different sorts of regularity, of connections between things, there might be. I don't think it is a common-

sense belief at all that there are just a few basic laws that completely control the behaviour of everything, so that everything
can be predicted if we know all the laws and the initial state of
everything. This is very much a speculation of physics.

Common sense will say that things are very often unpredictable. This is not because they are just irregular or wholly
arbitrary. It is rather because there are different sorts of laws
that can apply at any time, and which ones do apply can
depend on many factors, including free choices, reactions to
what is going on elsewhere, and so on. In other words, the
regularities leave room for creative changes, for new depar-
tures, for growth and inventiveness. We might say that
low-level regularities can be used or modified by higher-level
principles (so, when I play billiards, I use the laws of mechanics
to pot the ball, but I am thereby another, higher-level factor
that modifies the system without 'breaking' its laws). If the
laws did not operate predictably whenever there were no
outside influences, I could never know where the ball might go.
On the other hand, if I could not modify those laws by manipulating the cue, I would not be able to guide the ball at all. As
far as common sense goes, then, there must be laws generally
operating, but they must be modifiable by other sorts of influences – like my decisions, for example.

Now do the natural sciences suggest anything radically
different? At first sight, it looks as if they might. The physicist
Laplace is famous for his statement that, if he knew the first
state of the universe and all its laws, he could predict anything
that would ever happen afterwards.[8] But when you think about
it, that statement is quite obviously false, and only his great
reputation as a physicist stops us from seeing its absurdity. Just
think of one very simple case, where somebody thinks of a
theory that has never been thought of before – take Laplace's
theory as an example. One day Laplace thinks, 'Everything in
the universe is completely predictable'. And suppose that
thought has never occurred, in precisely the same way, ever
before. Can we predict what has never happened before, in
the whole history of the universe?

If you were a sophisticated philosopher, you might say that Laplace's thought was in fact caused by, or identical with (people are, significantly, not sure which) a certain state of Laplace's brain. And that brain-state, being purely physical, could have been predicted. That is because the brain consists of atoms, electrons, quarks or whatever, governed by various laws of interaction between them. If you can specify all the properties of quarks (now often thought to be the fundamental constituents of matter) and all the relations between all the quarks there are, you might be able to say what state all those quarks will be in, a few million years from now. Given enough information, you might be able to say what state Laplace's brain will be in, because that brain just consists of quarks and their properties.

Now it should be said that most modern physicists would even deny this – the principle of indeterminacy, used in quantum field theory, the chief way of explaining the world in terms of physics today, specifically denies that all quark states are predictable.[9] There is an essential indeterminacy about them, so that you could never be sure what they would all be like even in a few years' time, never mind a few million years. Physicists seem to have discovered that certain microscopic events are indeterminate in principle. There is a certain probability of their happening, but alternatives are always possible. General laws of interaction still apply, limiting the sorts of things that can happen. But the laws do not, apparently, determine that everything has to happen in just the way it does, and no other.

Nevertheless, let us ignore this very significant fact, and pretend that we could predict the position and properties of all the quarks in Laplace's brain. Would we then know what he was thinking? We would obviously not – unless we knew a law stating that a certain state of his brain always correlates with, or causes the thought that 'everything in the universe is completely predictable'. But how could we ever get such a law? We could not just magically intuit it out of the blue. We would have to get it, like all other laws of physics, from observation.

But the plain fact is that we could never have observed the thought, 'everything in the universe is completely predictable'. Because, until Laplace thought it, it had never occurred before, in the whole history of the universe. Therefore we could not know any law stating that such a thought would always be produced by the position of quarks in a certain central nervous system.

This, it seems to me, is a conclusive proof that not everything we know to be true about the universe is predictable from knowledge of a certain set of laws and the initial state of the universe. In general, if there are ever any new thoughts, or any sorts of things that have never happened before in the universe, then these things are in principle unpredictable by natural science (except as a sort of guess about the future, based on how things have gone in the past). Even if we could predict Laplace's brain, we could never predict his thoughts. That is obvious when you think about it – because, if you could predict new thoughts before they happened, then they wouldn't be new. If I predict Beethoven's Ninth Symphony before he writes it, then he needn't bother to write it, since it will already exist in my prediction. But that is totally absurd. So it is obvious that the universe contains a great many – in fact, an infinite number – of quite new, original, unpredictable things and states.

It would be very odd to suppose that all these unpredictable occurrences were totally without any effect on the rest of the world. It is sometimes said that thoughts cannot have causal effects on matter, because of the dogma that material objects constitute a complete, closed system. But this would conflict with another dogma of science, that every occurrence influences every other, in some way, however small. And it also seems to conflict with the well-established scientific principle that every action produces a reaction, so that you do not get one-way chains of causality, in nature, disappearing into nothing.[10] So, if we allow thoughts and feelings to be real, we are in essence saying that their reality has some effects on other real occurrences, including brain-states. These effects will clearly not be describable under universal laws, because of their uniqueness and originality. But is it really plausible to think that, whenever x affects y, it must be because of some universal law? Could there not be other forms of influence, which are intelligible without being deterministic? And do we not already have a perfectly good model for them, in conscious, purposive causes, which are not simply reducible to unconscious and mechanistic ones?[11]

Remember that the basic question we are asking is whether scientific method rules out any talk of purpose in the universe, and especially in the evolution of life. Jacques Monod, the French biologist, in his book, *Chance and Necessity*, says that the whole of science in fact depends upon the 'postulate of objectivity', which is the postulate that knowledge can never be reached by regarding phenomena in terms of purpose.[12] He goes on to say that pure chance, which is absolutely blind, is the source of every innovation in the universe. And this, he writes, 'is today the sole conceivable hypothesis, the only one compatible with observed and tested fact'.[13] I am suggesting that this opinion is quite false, and is not confirmed by the present state of science at all.

It may well be true that the procedures of natural science, which are basically analytical and quantitative, are not well suited to the discovery of purposes. The natural sciences succeed by measuring exactly, by specifying qualities precisely and by formulating laws of interaction mathematically. They are ideally suited to uncovering the regularities that govern the interactions of material particles when they are not modified by other influences. The idea of purpose has more to do with value, with the direction towards a desired end-state, and with quasi-intelligent control. The sciences simply do not deal with these things; they are not, in their present form, suited to do so. The postulate of objectivity may indeed be a good working principle, showing what sort of studies are most likely to lead to the discovery and control of the mechanisms of nature. It is rather like saying, 'Don't try to apply scientific techniques where they won't apply. Stick to studying the mechanisms.'

That doesn't mean there isn't anything else in the world, only that the natural sciences are not the proper disciplines to deal with those other things.

It is quite obvious that there are many other things in the world. There are feelings, thoughts, evaluations and whole bodies of theory and understanding of other people, the arts and human existence. There are all the things the humanities deal with — literary and art and music criticism, history, economics, sociology and the more interesting parts of human psychology, philosophy and theology — all these studies are not exact and quantitative. But they enlarge human understanding and knowledge. There is a short and simple proof that some knowledge can only be reached by regarding phenomena in terms of purpose. If I want to know the causes of the First World War, I can only gain any knowledge of that if I consider the purposes of many of the politicians and generals of the time. If I ignore all those purposes, and confine myself to a study of the chemical interactions taking place at that time, I will never gain any relevant knowledge of the First World War, as a piece of human history. Even if I could give you every chemical interaction that ever occurred, I would still lack knowledge of the most important thing — the history of the war. I could almost certainly not even deduce that there was a war on, if all I knew was the chemical interactions and nothing else.

All we have to say then is that there is plenty of knowledge that is not scientific knowledge — human knowledge of many sorts. This would be perfectly obvious, if people of the prestige of Monod had not frightened us into doubting it. Even if I know all about physics and chemistry, there are millions of things I still do not know. I may be the best physicist in creation, and not understand other people one little bit.

So, when Monod says that chance is the only hypothesis compatible with science, he is really only saying that, when the natural sciences cannot give a completely determined account of everything that happens — and they cannot — they have nothing else to appeal to in their system. So they call what is left over 'chance', the inexplicable. Now it is essential to point out that this is simply a counsel of despair, an admission of failure. It is not a startling new truth about the world. As Monod himself says, 'It is obviously impossible to imagine an experiment proving the non-existence anywhere in nature of a purpose'.[14] And it is impossible to prove that events which are inexplicable according to causal laws in the ordinary way are not results of purposive activity rather than chance – especially if they appear to result in the emergence of awareness and new, creative values.

It may sound a bit as if I am trying to insert purpose into the gaps left by science, which seems very unsatisfactory. But what I am actually doing is suggesting that it is science which, quite consciously and intentionally, leaves out purpose in its accounts of nature. So, of course, purpose will not be found in natural science. It will, however, be found in the world the sciences study, just as all the other personal or spiritual factors – consciousness, knowledge and value – will, too. Science cannot exclude it just by refusing to talk about it.

This means that the natural sciences do not give a complete account of the real world at all. And if we look carefully at what they do, we can see that they abstract from that real world certain features, which they then consider in isolation. The world of the natural sciences is a world of abstractions. We must never fall for the deception that the real world is just the world that science talks about, and nothing else. The real world is the world of sights, sounds, thoughts, feelings, people and animals; not the world of quarks and gluons or of molecules and amino acids. Of course, all those things are parts of the real world. But they are parts that have been artificially separated off by special, technical concepts, in the attempt to enable us to understand how it works. The world of the laws of physics is an abstract, other-things-being-equal world. That is, it considers only certain very abstract features of objects. It considers those properties that can be precisely described in exact definitions; properties that can be exactly measured, and show very regular law-like behaviour patterns. It then proposes a quite amazing thought-experiment, and says, 'If there was nothing in the world except these precisely described properties, interacting solely in accordance with these mathematically expressed laws of interaction, then we could make very reliable predictions about its subsequent states'.

But of course it is quite false that there is nothing in the world except properties that can be exactly described – how do you exactly describe your feelings at this moment, or the colours of the objects around you now? It is very probably false that objects act only in accordance with certain laws of physics. Any engineer who has tried to put a physical theory into practice knows that, unless you can control the situation very carefully – and thus exclude all unknown influences – the real world will hardly ever do exactly what we expect, in detail. It is only in the very carefully controlled conditions of laboratories that such things work out well – and even then, we have to allow for unnoticed factors. What experience seems to show is that objects left to themselves, without any unknown or external influences, will act in the regular ways described by the laws of physics. If they do not do so, we assume there must be a reason for it – the laws must have been modified (or the interactions of the objects must have been modified) by other causal factors. What these may be, we cannot always know. But there is no reason, except dogmatic unbelief, to exclude both Divine and human purposive action and direction from influencing the way the real world goes.

The knowledge of modern scientists is amazing, but so is the extent of their ignorance. If you read Monod's book, you see at once the immense contrast between his very confident assertions that science leaves no room for purpose, that 'objective (i.e. wholly non-purposive) knowledge is the only source of real truth',[15] and his frequent and honest admissions that present-day ignorance of developmental and metabolic mechanisms is very great. It can truly be said that the physical sciences are in an immense state of flux and change today; and it is almost impossible to foresee the shape they will take in a few years' time. In other words, this is not a time for scientific dogmas. It is a time for scientific openness, a time of great and exciting change in our most basic ideas. It is no longer quite so clear what the ultimate nature of matter is, or what its potentialities really are. Maybe the hard-line materialists find their position undermined by having to admit that they are no longer quite so sure what matter is. After all, what is the point of saying that everything is made of matter, if you do not know what that is? Is there any longer much point in calling yourself a materialist?

I have been concerned, in this chapter, to look at the claims made by some scientific biologists that man is not a rational soul with a unique dignity, the product of purposive creation by God or of a spiritual law of *karma*, which allots to each person the consequences of their own desires and acts. Thinkers like Jacques Monod claim that science now forces us to see human beings as just one sort of biological organism among others, not different in kind from them. And we are the results of a totally non-purposive process, of pure chance. Talk of the soul therefore becomes relegated to a poetic gloss on our prejudice in favour of the species we happen to belong to. It is without objective reference or true significance.

The findings of biology do lead us to change our view of human origins to a great extent. The theory that species have evolved from simpler forms does seem to be overwhelmingly probable. But, in looking at one traditional Christian account of the soul – that of Thomas Aquinas – we have seen that evolution does not in itself raise any new difficulties for Christian belief. If the human soul is, as Aquinas taught, the basic principle of a rational organism, the power of thought and understanding, then it can easily be seen as developing continuously from lower, non-rational or non-cognitive, forms of life. In modern terminology, we might say that, when the brain reaches a certain stage of complexity, the power of conceptual thought, of reasoning and thinking, begins to exist; and that is when a rational soul begins to be. The rational soul is that which has the power of understanding. We may not be able to tell with any certainty where such a capacity exists: does it exist in babies, in higher animals, in possible future computers? I think that today we might wish to see all life as having an important spiritual dimension, and not make such a clear distinction between humans and other organisms, just because humans are capable of abstract reasoning. Yet human persons certainly have a more developed capacity for moral choice than most other organisms known to us on this planet. This is a quite new and distinctive capacity in the story of earthly evolution. Whatever possesses it is importantly different in kind from other things that do not possess it. Evolution is such that it results in the genesis of beings possessing rational souls. We assume that members of the human species possess such souls; but other organisms may do so as well. The important point is that all rational souls do possess a special dignity and status because of that fact.

Most medieval thinkers in Judaism, Christianity and Islam accepted a view of the soul rather like that of Aquinas. When they said that the rational soul (which Aquinas was quite happy to call 'the mind' or 'the intellect') is incorporeal and substantive and immortal, we might best rephrase this today by saying that the subject of consciousness, of thought, understanding and knowledge, is known to itself in a quite unique way. It is known, not through the use of sense-organs, but by introspection. Although it needs some form of embodiment to have things to think about, it is separable from any particular body, and could exist in an imperfect way without it. Perhaps the best example is in dreaming, when I at least imagine myself continuing to exist, though not in this particular body. The soul, being a subject of rational consciousness, could exist without the particular body it informs. In other words, once the evolutionary process has generated a subject of rational consciousness, that subject is then capable of independent existence, or of existence in a different embodiment. It is, as Aquinas put it, a 'subsistent form'; it is essentially the form of some body, but it is capable of existing on its own. That view expresses very well the belief that I can survive the death of my body, that I might have a new and more perfect form of embodiment hereafter. This is, of course, true of any rational soul, whatever its body now happens to look like. So, while modern biology throws new light on the nature of the soul, it does not in fact undermine the idea of the soul as a quite distinctive sort of existence, with an importance far transcending that of any lumps of unconscious matter, however complicated.

I have spoken of what might be called the semitic view of the soul – that which is found in the great traditions of Judaism, Christianity and Islam. But in other world traditions very similar things could be said. The Indian traditions, for example, think of the soul ('jiva') as a sort of 'subtle body' that endures when the gross physical body dies. It has the characteristics of understanding and feeling, and it grows and develops over time. For the doctrine of rebirth, the soul may take different forms of embodiment; and this is not in fact so very different from the semitic belief in a 'resurrection' of the body as may at first appear. For both views, it is important that the soul has some form of embodiment and expression, and it lives beyond the death of this physical body. Of course the question of the ultimate destiny of the soul is a very complex one; the Indian traditions tend to look for an ultimate state in which individual personality as we know it is transcended in a non-dual unity of consciousness and bliss; whereas the semitic traditions speak rather of a growth into fuller relationship with God. Yet both would admit that such ultimate matters are hard to speak of; and what is of immediate importance for both is the status of the soul now and its immediate destiny. All the main religious traditions agree that the soul is not just a material product of mechanisms of random mutation, and that the whole process of biological evolution can be seen as a purposive process for giving rise to souls embodied in the way we now experience them.

Looking at the broad process of cosmic evolution it is hard to avoid the impression that the whole process of evolution is purposive. By the operation of a few simple laws, it results in the origin of new and uniquely valuable beings – souls, or subjects of rational consciousness. We have to examine the claims of biologists like Monod that modern science rules out purpose from the universe. What I have suggested is that biology cannot deny the existence of purpose in the universe; all it can do is to ignore its possible existence, and refuse to consider it. That is what Monod calls 'the postulate of objectivity'. It has been a most useful working principle for biologists, helping them to concentrate on mechanisms without being sidetracked by considerations of value or purpose. But modern biology is in fact much more aware of the very tentative and speculative nature of its fundamental postulates than Monod sometimes admits. It is not at all certain that adequate explanations can finally be achieved using present assumptions and techniques. It takes a very bold speculation to say that biology can now rule out purpose because it has the adequate explanation for all life. You might say it takes a bold speculation to assert the existence of the soul, too. But on the contrary, we are more certain of the distinctive existence of our own rational consciousness than we are of the truth of any wide-ranging theories of biology. The soul is known directly by each of us. It would take a virtually irrefutable biological theory to make us deny it, and there are no such theories in modern biology.

But we don't have to point simply to the uncertainty of some assumptions in biology. We can say that, in principle, biology cannot discover purpose, because it rules it out of consideration, as a matter of methodology. New and unpredictable things do happen in the universe, and they include many facts about the human soul. There are hundreds of truths about the world that science can never predict, which are in fact never even mentioned in scientific theories. If that is true, how could we ever be sure that all these facts came about purely by chance? Only by accepting a dogma that whatever science cannot explain either does not exist or has no explanation – so it is 'pure chance'. In this situation, it is perfectly plausible for the religious believer to say that, if science rules out purpose by definition, and then finds that there are many things it cannot explain, one very obvious thing to think is that it is precisely the bits science has left out that we need to bring back in again. Biology does a magnificent job of analysing the mechanisms of inheritance and molecular construction. In doing so, it does not need to refer to purpose or value at all. But there is no justification for saying that it eliminates purpose from the world. All we need to resist is the idea that any natural science gives the whole, complete and exhaustive truth about the real world. Biology can show us how the process of evolution works. It cannot, and does not, try to show us what the process is for, or what its purpose is. It cannot even tell us – and again, it does not try to tell us – some of the most important things about the process (for example, that it issues in the existence of rational souls).

Jacques Monod writes: 'Modern man turns towards science, or rather against it, now seeing its terrible capacity to destroy not only bodies but the soul itself.'[16] There is a battle for the soul, for the idea of the soul, in modern culture. But it is not a battle between science and religion. It is a battle between those who seek to extend proper biological and scientific methods and conclusions beyond their proper sphere, and those who are concerned to affirm the dignity and purpose of human life. The next stage of the argument must be with those who misapply the arguments of biology and related disciplines, to suggest that man is no more than a biological phenomenon, and his morality and religion no more than a set of instinctual or imprinted behaviour patterns. Once more, it will prove to be in the interests of scientific truth and accuracy to confine scientific statements to their own important but limited sphere, and to resist all attempts to make a particular science the arbiter of truth and falsehood for the whole of human life.

3

THE REDUCTION
OF MORALS
TO BIOLOGY

THE UNIQUENESS OF HUMAN NATURE is under attack from many biologists and ethologists – students of animal behaviour – who wish to stress that humans are just animals like other species. Thus they do not have a special value and dignity that separates them from other species, and we cannot regard them as especially important, spiritually or morally. Of course it would be quite wrong to think that only human persons were of value. But religions have regarded them as of special value, if only because they can realize their responsibility for the guardianship of animals and the environment and thus have a role as trustees of the planet. The biological attack, on the other hand, regards humans as governed by instinct and impulse, just like animals rather low on the evolutionary scale, and so deprives them of their responsibility for the world. It is rather ironic that it is through the use of those intellectual powers that are so well developed in the human species that thinkers have come to deny any special significance to human life. New sciences of ethology and ecology have grown up to study the relation of organisms to their environment. Animal behaviour is studied and used to illumine aspects of human behaviour. The phenomenon of morality is understood after the pattern of the social behaviour of other animals, especially the higher primates. There is, of course, nothing at all wrong with these sciences. They have the capacity to illuminate and extend our knowledge in very beneficial ways. The trouble comes when their findings are generalized outside their proper sphere of application, and made to give a pattern for understanding the whole of human life. That is when the attack on human nature is apt to begin, and that is where it must be resisted.

A recent widely read book was entitled *The Naked Ape*. It was written by a respected zoologist, and it is a brilliant, entertaining and illuminating study of how human behaviour can be re-interpreted in terms of animal behaviour. But it does have the quite conscious aim of dethroning human beings from their evolutionary pedestal. Far from being seen as just a little lower than the angels, or an immortal soul enshrined in a suitably formed body, man is now seen as just a little less obviously hairy than the ape, or a biological biped burdened with an imperfectly functioning brain. The short passage dealing with religion gives a good idea of the approach.

Religion is seen as a 'strange pattern of animal behaviour',[1] in which animals make rather exaggerated and prolonged submissive displays before bits of rock, writing or images of various sorts. This strange behaviour is accounted for as a tribal token of total submission to an all-powerful, dominant member of the group. But, since we see only too well the frailties of our fellows, this dominant member becomes an invisible God, and our submissive behaviour proves to be 'immensely valuable as a device for aiding social cohesion'.[2] So religion has played an important part in our evolution, by helping social cohesiveness, which has enabled us to survive in our world. But it almost goes without saying that all the particular beliefs are false. 'None of these gods exist in a tangible form', writes the author, Desmond Morris, so 'why have they been invented?'[3] It is assumed that the gods have been invented; that it is their function that is important; that the question of truth – of whether our 'invented theories' correspond to any objective reality – is not even worth raising.

Morris does not spend very long talking about morality, either. But it is clear that human morality will not be seen as a perception of moral claims made upon us, so that our response to them determines our eternal destiny. Rather, morality will be seen as a set of social behaviour patterns which, perhaps, have a social cohesion value or which are conducive to the better survival of our species. The way to look at morality is as a biological mechanism that has been conducive to our survival, not as a set of commanding moral rules. When we do this, we may find that many traditional moral attitudes – founded on a view of man as a spiritual soul who should be able to master his physical urges completely – seem to become absurd or even dangerous.

Konrad Lorenz is an ethologist who has written quite extensively about morality, from the point of view of his own discipline. In reading his work, we can see how traditional morality might come to seem impractical and ineffective. For some traditional moralities condemn all aggressive and lustful behaviour, as something we should be able to control. We are guilty if we cannot control it, and so we try to repress or deny knowledge of our own lust and aggression. Yet our morality is still enormously inefficient, because it has totally and obviously failed to bring about a significant change in human behaviour. The more men have talked about total self-sacrifice, the more they seem to have practised horrifying intolerance and institutional aggression.

The trouble has been, perhaps, that we have not appreciated the true biological and quite natural bases of behaviour that we share with other animals, and which originate in our own pre-history. Lorenz, in his book *On Aggression*,[4] shows how aggression is not some sinful aberration humans never had until they fell into sin. It is, on the contrary, an entirely natural, even an essential, characteristic for the survival of a relatively soft-skinned, slow-moving animal like man, in a world of threatening animal rivals. It is entirely understandable that this aggressiveness, which was once so necessary to ensure our very survival, should remain and become troublesome to us after the real need for it has disappeared.

Lorenz points out that inter-specific aggression, between individuals of different species, is always related to food and survival requirements. But intra-specific aggression, between members of the same species, is also related to the preservation of the species. It performs the function of marking out territorial boundaries and so of spreading the species more or less evenly over the available environment. It helps to ensure the survival of the strongest members of a group, which is useful for defence against competing groups. It ensures the strongest protection for young children. And it establishes a ranking order in the tribe, which is conducive to the establishment of a complex social order in which division of labour can take place. Thus the group as a whole can become more efficient in the techniques of survival and adaptation.

It is obvious that aggression can get out of hand and become counter-adaptive to the survival of the species, especially when environmental conditions change greatly or rapidly. But it is a primary instinctual drive, which has had an essential part to play in the evolution of man. This fact has, perhaps, not been sufficiently recognized in traditional moral views, for which aggression might be seen as something evil, for which each person is individually responsible. Acceptance of a biological view of man as the product of animal evolution makes it impossible to accept either the radical evilness of such factors as aggression and lust in human life, or an absolute moral responsibility and guilt for possessing such drives at all. Instead, they can be accepted as quite natural parts of our animal inheritance. And when we see that, we may be able to set about dealing with them more rationally and successfully. Instead of repressing them and trying to pretend they are not as strong as they are, we can admit their compelling force and seek to direct them to constructive ends – perhaps by some form of chemical control. What we need is a detailed empirical study of human nature from a biological standpoint, so that we can discover the forms and limits of our instinctual drives. Then we can look for ways of modifying these drives so that the human species can develop in security and harmony of interests.

Some things in this account strike me as being importantly right, and others as being importantly wrong. It is true, for instance, that Christians cannot stick to a literal interpretation of human beings having 'fallen' from some absolutely innocent state – a state in which, evidently, lions ate grass and the ground did not need to be cultivated to produce food. That is a myth, a story that is not literally true, but makes a point – about creation and about human nature – in a poetic, allegorical way. We have to say that *homo sapiens* has evolved, and that, if the biologists say so, there were other species, like the *australopithecines*, much more like man than like present-day apes, who became extinct millions of years ago. We can still readily distinguish *homo sapiens* as a distinct species, but we cannot say that he is totally different in kind from all other possible species of animal.

Who, then, was the first man? Well, of course, we will never know, exactly. But it must be the case that some animal, at some point in time, for the very first time on earth developed a sense of self-awareness, of moral responsibility, of spiritual understanding. And we can say that, however primitive these things were, that animal was a person. In other words, it is not strictly the fact that we belong to the species *homo sapiens* that gives us a unique status and dignity. It is because we are persons, beings of spiritual self-awareness, of that specific sort of rational consciousness which, in the previous chapter, I called 'the soul'. Persons undoubtedly began to exist on earth at a certain point in time. When that happened, man came into being – for man or *homo sapiens* is the form personhood takes, the only form we really can be sure of, on this earth.

In this context, it hardly makes sense to say that the first man was created perfect. At least, he would not be wholly without lust or aggression, which had helped to get him so far along the evolutionary road. I think it makes perfectly good sense, however – and I think it is a reasonable interpretation of what the myth of 'the fall' means – to say something like this: when the first men began to feel that sense of distinctively moral claim, they were able either to respond or to turn away from it. Perhaps it asked them not to be quite so aggressive, or not to let their lust take an unthinking, automatic course. They had some measure of moral responsibility, however restricted. It was their failure to respond to the moral claim, when they could have done so, that was 'the fall'. For, from that point, their turning away influenced others, especially their children, so that the human race was never again free from that sense of moral failure that is such a large part of what we call 'sin'.

We can accept Lorenz's plea to recognize lust and aggression as natural drives, then. We can be grateful for his reminder that we should not expect people to be angels, or to feel guilty for bits of their nature they cannot help. But we should begin to resist when he implies that all there is to morality is a set of survival-orientated imprinted drives, which we may in future be able to modify by behavioural control mechanisms. Recognition of a moral claim and the birth of moral responsibility are precisely those points when, for a religious person, a human being begins to take on a unique dignity and importance. We cannot and should not reduce that to the same sort of behavioural stimulus and response that characterizes so much animal behaviour.

Yet Lorenz writes, 'In principle there is no difference between the rigidity with which we adhere to our early toilet-training and our fidelity to the national or political norms and rites to which we become object-fixated in later life'.[5] Again, 'Man's fidelity to all his traditional customs is caused by creature habit and by animal fear at their infraction'.[6] In case there is any misunderstanding of his position here, he makes it quite blunt and clear very soon: 'Oaths cannot bind, nor agreements count, if the partners to them do not have in common a basis of ritualised behaviour standards at whose infraction they are overcome by . . . magic fear'.[7]

Morality itself, he seems to be saying, is a matter of rigid, ritualized behaviour patterns, which are quite non-rational in origin. They survive solely as inhibitory mechanisms that have been conducive to species-survival. We adhere to morality largely because we cannot help it. We are rigidly 'object-fixated' and conditioned. We have a 'magic' – non-rational – fear of disobeying these repressive rules. We do not obey moral rules *because* we see that they are right, or even that they are conducive to survival. That would be much too conscious and rationalized a procedure. Such rules inhibit our natural desires out of a combination of fear and conditioning.

'Morality', then, is the name of one among many instinctive behaviour patterns and inhibitions that characterize the human and some other animal species. It is, in itself, no more or less important than other human drives. Man has no rational choice of what these drives shall be: they are biologically pre-determined. Moreover, on a purely biological level it is incorrect to speak of goals or purposes at all. There are no real goals in nature, so it is incorrect to speak of nature, whether human or animal nature, as setting goals that man must try to implement – goals of survival or development, for instance. If men speak of 'survival' as a goal of human endeavour, therefore, they cannot claim that this is somehow a goal of the evolutionary process itself. Biologically speaking, survival and adaptation are by-products of 'moral' inhibitions, which happen to have been selected by random mutation; survival is certainly not the 'purpose' of morality.

This general view is made even clearer in the work of E. O. Wilson, author of *Sociobiology*, an ambitious work that looks forward to an explanation of all social behaviour in terms of its biological bases. He writes, 'In a Darwinist sense the organism does not live for itself. Its primary function is not even to reproduce other organisms, it reproduces genes, and it serves as their temporary carrier . . . the organism is only DNA's way of making more DNA.'[8] Genes are fundamental self-replicating mechanisms in all living things, and it is the genes that are selected for survival by their favourable propagation in various environments, as a result of random mutations. The organisms are just the carriers of the genes, which proliferate maximally under certain conditions – but entirely without purposive direction. It would be a fundamental mistake to see the individual or the species as somehow trying or struggling to survive. All that is really happening is that certain behavioural complexes are favourable to the transmission of specific genes; and those are the ones that get transmitted. Evolution has to be seen in terms of differential rates of gene replication, and not in terms of the attempt of individuals or species to survive.

It is hard to see where morality, religious belief, or indeed any kind of rational belief fits into this scheme at all. It is certainly illuminating to discover more about the undoubted genetic bases of human behaviour. But reservations begin to appear when reason, freedom and moral endeavour seem to be explained in terms only of non-purposive genetic processes. And alarm bells certainly begin to ring when Wilson says, 'Altruism is conceived as the mechanism by which DNA multiplies itself . . . spirituality becomes just one more Darwinian enabling device'.[9] All our highest ideals and most difficult aspirations, the agonies of spirit and the heroisms of moral commitment, stand revealed as mechanisms for the multiplication of DNA. The suggestion is so extraordinary that we might wonder if any rational person could make it seriously. But Wilson presses on: 'The hypothalamic-limbic complex of a highly social species, such as man . . . has been programmed to perform as if it knows that its underlying genes will be proliferated maximally only if it orchestrates behavioural responses that bring into play an efficient mixture of personal survival, reproduction and altruism.'[10] And, in another work, *On Human Nature*, he presses home the point: 'Beliefs are really enabling mechanisms for survival . . . thus does ideology bow to its hidden masters the genes.'[11]

The basic intellectual defect with theories of this sort is that they deny the most certain and obvious observable facts and try to replace them with a very general, speculative and abstract theory. That theory is one that proves extremely useful for certain rather limited and precise areas of study – in this case, the cellular and developmental mechanisms of organisms. Even there, of course, there are huge areas of ignorance and speculation. Nevertheless, present genetic theories do possess an elegance, simplicity and explanatory power which, if not complete, is very impressive. They are at the very least useful tools for research and experimentation. We need to remember, however, what happened to Newtonian physics when Faraday began to study electromagnetism, and how the very foundations of physics were shaken by quantum mechanics and field-theory. Experimental scientists, of all people, should be constantly aware of how tentative and revisable and incomplete their theories are; how limited in their ability to encompass reality.

In a well-known aphorism, Einstein declared, 'As far as the laws of mathematics refer to reality, they are not certain; and as far as they are certain, they do not refer to reality'.[12] That is, all our scientific theories are abstract approximations to a reality that they cannot completely grasp in their full nature. Niels Bohr, another great nuclear physicist, said, 'Isolated material particles are abstractions'.[13] The physicists are well aware that their fundamental concepts are both revisable and incomplete – they are embodied in mathematical models that can never encompass every aspect of the world, but which succeed precisely because they are abstractions and generalizations. They deal only with the general aspects of phenomena, not with the unique and new. And their explanatory value is limited, in the real world, by the extent to which, as models, they are forced to abstract from the rich detail of actual life and experience.

How far physicists' awareness of the partial and tentative nature of scientific models seems to be from the dogmatic and imperialistic claims of some sociobiologists! If a scientific theory is a partial, abstract and useful tool for understanding, it must finally be judged by its ability to help us to understand the data we start from. It cannot ever undermine those data; even less can it end by denying their very existence. Genetic theories are, after all, abstract, generalized and mathematically specified models of the real world, using certain very precisely defined technical concepts. The aim of these abstract models is to help us to understand organic and human life. Something has gone drastically and fundamentally wrong when we begin to talk about the model as though it were the reality, and about the real world it should be helping us to understand as though it did not even exist. Sociobiology, in its very brief and almost wholly speculative accounts of ethical behaviour, is an attempt to replace the certain by the tentative, the concrete by the abstract, the particular by the general, and actual experience by pure theory. It is one modern equivalent of those pure theoreticians who refused to look through Galileo's telescope to see the facts, in case the sight spoilt their theory. Modern science has progressed by the belief that even the most beautiful theories need to fit the observed facts; and if they do not, they should be modified.

When certain biologists start talking about human beliefs in terms of genetic theory they are, first of all, misunderstanding the revisable and abstract character of their own theories; secondly, they are misapplying those theories wildly outside the sphere in which they are genuinely useful explanatory tools; and thirdly, they are ignoring a first principle of scientific method, which is to look clearly at the facts, and not be content with mere theories. Now the facts in question are some of the most clearly and certainly known to us. They are the facts of moral experience, of rational thought, of purpose and intention in human affairs. Any theory that makes these facts magically disappear, and be transformed into something else, unexperienced, unconscious, not even thought of, must be wrong.

And that mistake has moral consequences of very great importance, because in the end these theorists are going to start making recommendations about what morality or religion should become in future. Once, according to them, we have understood it, we can deal with it more efficiently. As Wilson writes, 'A science of sociobiology, if coupled with neurophysiology, might transform the insight of ancient religions into a precise account of the evolutionary origin of ethics and hence explain the reasons why we make certain moral choices instead of others'.[14] For this reason, he says, 'The time has come for ethics to be removed temporarily from the hands of the philosophers and biologicised'.[15] I very much doubt if they would ever want it back, if this terrible thing happened. But Wilson is optimistic. 'A genetically accurate and hence completely fair code of ethics must wait', he says, for the complete decoding of the neural basis of ethical judgements in the brain.[16]

Evidently, what is supposed to happen is that we will be able to give a complete scientific account of why we behave morally as we do. Then, by adjustment of the brain or the genes, we will be able to control behaviour more efficiently in future. The aim is clear. Complete explanation gives complete control. When we have explained man, we can control him. But who is the 'we'? And how will we control man? Well, at least we will have no anti-scientific notions of human freedom and responsibility. We will see that man is, in the title of a recent book by the behavioural psychologist B. F. Skinner, *Beyond Freedom and Dignity*. We will see that 'man is not a moral animal in the sense of possessing a special trait or virtue; he has built a kind of social environment which induces him to behave in moral ways'.[17] Then we can change that environment, and induce him to behave in any way we want.

But if this is the way things are seen, can morality survive? It is obvious that religion cannot, since all the gods have been invented, and obviously do not exist (that is obvious, because they are not contained in any scientific theory, and scientific theories are supposed to tell us the whole truth about the world). Yet we may need to have something that can carry out the functions religion used to possess – namely, to enforce the most vital interests of the group and aid its social cohesion. The most obvious candidate would seem to be an absolute dictatorship, backed by all the resources of genetics and biology; and no doubt the chosen dictator will be some sociobiologist.

But at this point a strange thing usually begins to happen. When a biologist speaks of using the knowledge made available by the rapid progress of his science in order to further human interests or social cohesion and development, he at once jumps right outside his own scheme of explanation, and starts using purposive recommendations for action. Moreover, his purposes (or the ones he says he has) are usually fairly moderate, liberal and kindly, just those of benevolent scientists in a liberal democratic culture. What an amazing coincidence! In fact, this sort of biologist (and I should emphasize that I am only speaking of those who claim that their theories embrace the whole of human experience, not of the ordinary, practising, straightforward scientist) is virtually schizophrenic in his inter- pretation of reality. On the one hand, he says that morality is not a rational, purposive phenomenon at all. It is a set of inhibitory mechanisms that had high survival value in the past. On the other hand, he says that his findings can help us to implement a new, more rational (or even 'fairer') morality that will enable us to achieve the basic purposes of human nature. But where did this sudden introduction of a 'rational or fair' morality come in? Why should it be a subject of concern at all? Is it not precisely one of those things that has been shown to be simply an enabling mechanism for survival? Can we seriously continue to speak of reason and fairness, once we have uncovered the real roots of all human action?

After all, if what these biologists say is right, morality is no longer a phenomenon giving man a unique dignity as a free rational agent, with final responsibility for his own destiny. On the contrary, it is a set of non-rational conditioned behaviour patterns, some of them silly, arbitrary or pointless, but con- tributing on the whole to the cohesion and survival of the human species. In other words, morality is not the highest point of conscious human development; it is an authoritarian but normally irremovable hangover from the repressive taboos of primitive tribes.

The person who believes this, and believes it of all morality, not inconsistently exempting so-called 'rational morality' from this description, has surely moved beyond morality altogether. Whatever he thinks and however he acts, he will no longer be able to think of morality as a set of finally and absolutely important obligations that it is rational and human to obey. It follows, therefore, that when he does not feel himself to be totally conditioned to a certain form of action, he will not rationally appeal to moral considerations as a reason for acting. To the extent that a man is not wholly and effectively conditioned by his biological past, he will be free of those moral constraints by which men have felt themselves bound throughout the history of western culture. This is a sort of liberation, or liberation from primitive, non-rational, repressive behaviour patterns. It is a liberation made possible by scientific discovery. But, like Nietzsche's liberation from objective moral values, it turns out to be a liberation into despair.

For, as individuals, we have no possible interest in the survival of particular genes; and, indeed, their survival is not a rationally chosen purpose in any sense. We must continue to have purposes and to act more or less rationally, because we simply cannot regard ourselves as scientific objects all the time. Whatever we believe about ourselves as being biologically explicable, we will have to go on living with others, loving or hating, enjoying or disliking, just as before. Yet there will be a difference. We cannot proceed with our lives in these two quite distinct, and indeed contradictory, departments. In one of them, the scientific department, we are non-purposive and non-rational carriers of randomly selected, self-replicating genes. In the other, everyday-life department, we have purposes, interests, desires and needs that we consider important. Can we hold these two together?

Only by not thinking about it. We simply cannot avoid the questions, 'What is it reasonable for me to do?' 'What purposes is it reasonable for me to have and pursue?' And to answer these questions we will naturally look to see what human nature really is and what its possibilities are. If we then find that many of our behaviour patterns are conditioned by exigencies of the past; that what we have often thought of as specially important, 'moral', obligations, can be best accounted for in terms of genetically imprinted inhibitory mechanisms; and if we are able to modify these by some form of bioengineering or environmental structuring – then these moral norms will lose their special binding force. We will be free to do whatever we want, unbound by moral inhibitions, considerations of fairness, rationality or anything else.

But there is a self-destructive paradox in this view. For what is being said is, 'If you truly *understand* human behaviour, then you will see that it is *unreasonable* to be bound by any special moral sense, because it is only an inhibitory mechanism'. However, this understanding of truth and this idea of reason-ableness are themselves biological mechanisms also. They have no special spiritual status; like morality, they too must be seen as 'enabling mechanisms for gene replication'. They lose their normative force, too. Why bother to understand or to be reasonable? Why pursue truth or rationality?

Now this is a very serious question, for we cannot divorce morality from truth and reason. In fact, we might very well say that morality is reasonable action, in the light of rationally understood truth. And we might say that the disinterested pursuit of truth is itself a normative, a moral obligation. It is one of our chief moral obligations to seek truth and to be rea-sonable. But if morality no longer has any binding force, then there is no particular reason to seek truth.

That is exactly the view that is taken in some totalitarian societies. Truth is a matter of social control; it is not an absolute, so it can be manipulated by societies or groups for their own ends. Where morality, truth and reason have all lost their force, all that is left is the blind struggle for power – a return to the pre-rational conditions of nature from which human civilization has been so painfully attempting to climb. It is sad indeed if reason ends by undermining itself, by indulging in a sort of suicide that declares itself to be non-existent. There is no escaping the paradox of this view. For, even as reason declares itself to be powerless, it is the power of reason that is making the declaration, which is taking authority on itself to declare this view to be true. It is, after all, being said that it is the final truth about human life that final truth is unimportant. If we try to escape this paradox by denying that we are telling the truth, by denying any interest in the truth, then that escape can indeed be effected. But it can only be effected if we stop thinking and talking. The moment we begin to think again, we are, by definition, following canons of reason in the attempt to state truths.

There is a huge amount at stake here, for the whole future of human life. Perhaps this issue is the deepest and most momentous that the human species now faces; for it affects our thoughts, our aspirations, our morale and self-understanding at its most basic levels. Are we going to move beyond freedom, reason, dignity and morality? Are we going to accept the rule of chance, of impulse, of feeling and of force? This would be the ultimate effect of accepting the 'biologicizing' accounts of human morality and of the human soul that we have looked at in this chapter. If that is what we *really* are, carriers of non-intentionally self-replicating genes, then our acceptance of that fact will destroy all that we have held distinctive and valuable in human life and history finally and ineluctably.

And yet that biologicizing account is self-refuting. It is so, precisely because it claims to be telling the truth, at last, about the human condition. It claims to be prepared to face up to that truth, whatever the consequences. It claims that we *should* – it would be *reasonable* to – modify human behaviour to take account of these facts. Truth, morality and reason are all appealed to as normative in the very setting out of the theory that is supposed to be undermining them.

It is very like the paradox of the person who says, 'All statements made by me are false'. If what he says is true, it must be false. So, when the biological moralist says that morality is just a set of imprinted behaviour patterns, and in the same breath recommends that we *ought* to face up to and accept this, because it is the truth, he is simply contradicting himself. The fact is that he has a morality himself; he is recommending it as a better one than what he thinks is the traditional morality. But when we ask him why it is better, his answer is that it is more rational or more fair. Lorenz speaks of 'our rational, responsible morality'; and Wilson writes of a possible 'completely fair code of ethics'. I do not suppose that any traditional moralist would complain about the ideas of responsibility and fairness; or think that his own moral code was either unfair or irresponsible. The ideas of fairness and responsibility, together with further ideas of sensitivity to others and self-realization, are central to morality, to what makes human life of distinctive worth. But those ideas do not derive simply from a study of how human behaviour has developed in the course of evolution. They develop from present reflection on human experience, on the distinctive nature of human persons and on those states and activities that are worth rational pursuit.

Of course, a study of human evolution will be relevant to moral reflection; no one would deny that. It can tell us more about human limitations and possibilities; it may help to prevent us being impossibly idealistic or unreasonably depressed about our own moral performance. But it will not tell us what morality is – any more than study of the development of chemistry out of alchemy will tell us what chemistry really is.

What the biologicists are doing is to commit what has been called the 'genetic fallacy'. This sounds a very apt name for them, but in fact it has nothing to do with genes at all. It is the mistake of thinking that you can understand what something is when you have seen how it has developed. In its most extreme and absurd form, it is the mistake of saying that what a thing now is *really*, is what it was when it began to develop.

We might think nobody would commit such a silly mistake. But it has been a constant feature of twentieth-century semi-scientific speculation. The first anthropologists who studied religion – people like Frazer in *The Golden Bough* – tended to argue that because, according to them, primitive religion was all fear and superstition, therefore that is what present-day religion really was. The biologicists do a similar sort of thing when they point to various animal modes of behaviour and say that this shows us what developed human behaviour really is. Seeing man as a naked ape is just one huge example of the genetic fallacy, of seeing the developed specimen as no more than its primitive ancestor. But, while it is very important to realize that Albert Einstein was once a baby, it is ludicrous to suggest that he really always was a baby. Moral ideas may have developed from animal behaviour patterns. But now, in the developed human species, they are quite different in kind. They are reflective, rational and conscious values, and it would be fatal to reduce them to what, in the course of evolution, they once developed from.

Moral ideas cannot, then, be derived solely from a study of animal or evolutionary biology. This conclusion is reinforced by the fact that various people who have tried to base a rational morality on the biological facts have arrived at very different conclusions. C. H. Waddington, a noted biologist, sees the evolutionary process as one that brings about increasing richness of consciousness and complexity of organization. So he sees the function of ethical systems as being to further this evolutionary advance at a conscious level.[18] But the equally eminent biologist T. H. Huxley, in a famous lecture on 'Evolution and Ethics', took a very different view. While agreeing that we ought to aim at social harmony and individual creativity, he considered that nature was cruel and purposeless, 'red in tooth and claw'. So man's duty is not to further the evolutionary trend, but to oppose it as well as he can.[19]

Other thinkers have agreed with this estimate that nature is an ugly, wasteful and haphazard process; but they have applauded this and sought to emulate it in human affairs. Thus Herbert Spencer held that the continual battle of evolution, in which the strong survive and the weak become extinct, justifies a *laissez-faire* policy in human affairs.[20] Harmony and integration are values of the weak; what really counts is strength, force and courage – and we can see how that view could be derived from a study of the evolutionary process, too.

It is obvious, then, that the process of evolution can be interpreted in different ways. And in any case, a study of it cannot determine whether we should oppose it or help it along. This strongly suggests that what the biological moralists are really doing is to impose their own moral ideals on the evolutionary process, rather than, as they claim, deriving moral ideas from the process itself. On the one hand, they claim to show that morality is not a rational purposive phenomenon at all. On the other hand, they say that their findings can help us to implement a new, more rational morality that can preserve and develop the human species – as though that species and its survival were of any importance in their biological scheme.

But the new 'evolutionary morality' they propose is nothing more than an uneasy compromise between what they think the traditional morality is and its total overthrow. They claim to understand human nature simply in terms of animal nature, thus eroding any sense of human distinctiveness and person-hood. They reduce the aims of morality to the minimal end of survival, thus depriving survival of any particular point or purpose beyond itself. And they recommend bioengineering as more efficient than moral exhortation, thus denying any impor-tance to human freedom and choice. What they have done is to reduce morality to its most minimal elements, and reduce the importance of moral endeavour and individual responsibil-ity virtually to zero. Yet they continue to talk of moral ends (even if the end is only that of the survival of the species) and of some sort of obligation to achieve that end.

The dilemma of this view can be put very sharply. If the biological account of morality is accepted in its entirety, we will have to give up all belief in moral ends, in absolute moral obligations. We will just have to talk about conditioning people to various forms of behaviour, and give up morality altogether. But if moral purposes and obligations are to be retained at all, the reduction of their difficulty and importance by the 'new morality' has no scientific basis; it cannot be derived from the factual study of biology alone. So it just expresses a determination to have an easier moral code and to reduce the importance of human freedom and dignity. We cannot accept the first half of this dilemma, for if we do we fall into self-contradiction. But if we accept the second half, we have to admit that these ethological and sociobiological studies, fascinating though they are, are not going to provide us with a satisfactory basis for morality.

What they have done, under the disguise of a scientific analysis of human behaviour, is to mount an attack upon the human soul by attacking that which is most distinctive of it and important to it, the sense of moral claim and responsibility, the sense of spiritual freedom and dignity, the sense of justice, honesty, fidelity and love. We have to say of this attack that either it is self-contradictory − since it holds that we *ought* to abandon all *oughts* − or it is simply a proposal to reduce morality to a set of rules for survival. Such a proposal has been made many times before; and it is, perhaps, the deepest form of atheism − the belief that we should just try to go on surviving, even though there is no real point in it. If we are to find something unique and worthwhile about the human soul, it will certainly not be in its biological survival value. As we have seen, by that criterion the genes themselves would easily win. It is by our moral and spiritual awareness, by our responsible and intelligent understanding, that we are distinguished as beings of dignity and freedom. I have been concerned to argue that there is nothing in the biological sciences, properly under-stood, to undermine this claim. The soul still stands, and indeed its distinctiveness is thrown into higher relief when we realize how human life itself would change and disintegrate if we did not know and accept it. But there is another sort of attack upon the soul that also threatens to undermine its uniqueness and dignity. It is an attack upon its basically spiritual nature, upon the authority of conscience and upon the whole idea of duty. The attack comes from certain thinkers who have been influenced by psychoanalysis, and it is to them that we must next turn.

4

THE ATTACK
ON CONSCIENCE

JUST AS DARWINISM made men aware in a new way of their kinship and continuity with the animal species and with the genetic origins of their present modes of behaviour, so the startling doctrines of Sigmund Freud made clear to men for the first time the unconscious motivations underlying much of their behaviour and the dependence of beliefs and attitudes upon specific types of development, training and experience in childhood.

Again, the new emphasis was on two major factors, development and continuity. The behaviour of the human adult was seen in the light of the young human's experiences. And mature behaviour was seen as continuous with immature and childhood behaviour. Moreover, man was treated completely as an object of the scientific attitude, an object causally determined like others, and capable of being understood and even controlled in an objective, dispassionate way. Psychoanalysis overcame the last resistance to the scientific attitude, the existence of private consciousness.

Philosophers since Descartes had regarded their own consciousness as known more certainly to them than anything else, as an indisputable feature of the world. But Freud's work seemed to show that in fact other people could tell what was in one's mind better than one could oneself – for the individual is subject to many illusions and deceptions about his own conduct. He also showed that there was no clear and decisive dividing-line between conscious and unconscious mental processes – so the mind could not be defined as that which was conscious. It is the mind that dreams, presumably, and yet we are rarely conscious of dreaming. Once men saw that the mind was not clearly knowable by introspection and not totally different in kind from non-mental existence, it came to seem not the rational moral agency it had been thought to be. It was rather the battleground of many diverse impulses and desires. The idea, deriving from Plato but somehow surviving at the back of people's minds, of a 'soul' or mental substance, which was somehow unfortunately trapped inside a gross physical body, could no longer survive.

We have already seen that the traditional idea of the soul in the semitic faiths, as I outlined it in its Christian form in Aquinas, was rather different from this Platonic idea. But the Christian idea, too, seemed to be threatened by Freud's suggestion that consciousness is an uncertain, flickering, untrustworthy and marginal phenomenon in the economy of the mind. For the place of rational or moral thought in determining human conduct will be much less important on such a view than on the traditional view, for which man freely and consciously chooses to be moral or immoral, selfish or altruistic. Indeed, Freud sometimes wrote as though all supposed reasons for acting were no more than rationalizations of primitive drives to sex, aggression or power, and as though all 'moral' conduct was a disguised form of self-interest. When it came to religious belief, he was quite unequivocally clear that it was an irrational phenomenon that could only be accounted for by a study of the pathology of the mind.

The most fundamental insight of the Freudian approach to the human mind is its insistence that all mental events are caused, and caused by processes largely unknown to the conscious mind or ego. Moral judgement is thus out of place. Just as the psychoanalyst gets the neurotic patient to recall all his experiences without passing moral judgement on them, so, when the causal determinants of human behaviour are known, moral judgement seems to be entirely out of place. Conscious reasoning is hardly, if ever, an effective determinant of behaviour. Man has to discover the motives of his own actions, just as he has to discover the sequence of causes in the external world. Whereas traditional morality sometimes seems to assume that man can overcome 'sinful dispositions' simply by taking thought and by strength of will, the findings of Freudian analysis suggest that men must accept their instinctive drives and attempt to integrate them so as to avoid neurosis or mental ill-health. The most reason can do is to check the worst conflicts that arise from the play of one's instincts. And even then it is far from efficient. We are all neurotics, and we must learn to live with that fact as best we can.

Sigmund Freud, born twelve years later than Nietzsche and forty-seven years later than Charles Darwin, started life as a neurologist who was primarily interested in the anatomy and physiology of the brain. He did in fact suggest at one time the hope that the long and arduous techniques of psychoanalysis might be more efficiently performed by surgical operations on the brain itself. He would probably not have opposed a view of the unconscious mental forces that identified them with specific neurophysiological processes in the brain. It is only an unfortunate matter of fact that neurosis has now to be treated by the long, not totally effective, and expensive method of analysis.

This method, developed by Freud in the teeth of great opposition from his colleagues, is basically a method of resolving crippling neuroses by the recall of repressed experiences. The whole mechanism of repression, resistance, transference and hysteria that the method unveiled does not, for Freud, have any particular spiritual import or significance. It may well be, in the end, a purely physiological mechanism, largely operative below the level of consciousness and resulting from inefficiency of the information-carrying equipment of the brain. But until we understand the mechanism of the brain better, the rather clumsy methods Freud and his followers evolved for dealing with neuroses and mental disorder will continue to be better than nothing. And, whether they prove to be finally inadequate accounts to explain the complex workings of the human brain or not, the changed understanding of human nature for which Freud has been largely responsible will remain of permanent significance.

The most obviously significant part of Freud's theory with respect to the phenomena of morality and religion is his teaching on the nature and function of the 'super-ego'. Quite early in his investigations into the genesis of neuroses – both by the method of recalling past experiences under hypnosis and by the technique of free association, in which the patient simply talks to a largely passive analyst – Freud found that many, if not most, of the childhood experiences that had been repressed into the unconscious, and were resistant to recall, expressed desires and emotions that were regarded by the patient as immoral and unacceptable. These impulses, which were primarily those of aggression and sex, were rejected by the patient in childhood, and repressed from consciousness. But they continued to operate, unrecognized, and sometimes found outlet in hysteria or obsessional neuroses. Freud found that the neuroses could be treated if the patient could be brought to recognize and accept the repressed impulses, instead of continuing to repress them.

Of course, neurotic patients were unaware that they were repressing any impulses at all. The whole process of repression was unconscious; and so at first Freud coined the term 'censor' to denote the unconscious mechanism of repression. But he later came to call it the super-ego; something higher than and controlling the ego, or conscious mind, whose operations are usually unknown by and unsuspected by the person concerned. The super-ego largely corresponds to what philosophers have called 'conscience'. It performs the same function of exercising moral control and guidance, and of arousing feelings of guilt or anxiety if one's moral code is contravened.

Freud pointed out that the operations of the super-ego were largely unconscious and not at all based on conscious reasoning. They could be repressive, stupid, rigid and infantile; and, by the irrational suppression of the natural forces of instinct, they were chiefly responsible for neuroses. In fact, Freud's discovery was that most neurotics were ill, not because they were morally inadequate in some way, but because they were too moral, too heavily repressed by their super-egos. So, as a result of psychoanalytic techniques, conscience came to be seen as a dangerous, irrational, clumsy and repressive mechanism that governed human conduct at a level below that of rational consciousness. Consequently, the task of analysis often was to loosen the hold of conscience and release people from the hold of their irrational guilt and anxiety. In short, it was to free people from the reign of morality, and of religion, which was used to give that morality even stronger supernatural sanctions.

Psychoanalysts will usually deny that they are concerned with morality at all, or with religious belief either. Their concern, they will say, is with mental health and neuroses. They seek to understand the mind and cure mental disease; they do not make moral recommendations or criticize particular moral views. This, however, is plainly false. As opposed to a view of conscience that sees it as the voice of God, or an infallible guide to conduct, a reliable judge of one's own moral performances and the just judge of one's own wrong-doing, Freudians point out that the super-ego originates in infantile experience; that it is often irrational or cruel and repressive; that it causes needless and crippling feelings of guilt, which need to be removed by acceptance of one's repressed 'bad' impulses. Naturally they will claim that these facts are medically ascertained, not just speculative opinions. They might be very largely correct. But they will still clearly be changing some conceptions of what morality is; and inevitably, therefore, they will challenge and reject some particular moral views – even if only the more censorious or peculiar ones.

But some people who have been influenced not only by Freud's eminently helpful and imaginative medical practices, but also by the very wide-ranging and speculative theories he formed to try to explain those practices, go much further. They may find themselves rejecting the phenomenon of morality altogether. For, if there are any moral absolutes, conscience is the faculty that apprehends them. Yet Freud seems to have exposed the super-ego as a natural mechanism that is very ineffective, may cause more harm than good, and is often a cause of mental illness. Conscience-morality is thus seen as a mechanism for influencing human conduct, in what are no doubt generally survival-enhancing ways for the species (or, to be more exact, for the genes), but as one that is both inefficient and obsolete, now that it has been seen through. If human conduct is to be influenced in future, therefore, it will not be by means of morality. How it will be influenced is another matter; but at least appeal to moral absolutes or to the 'dictates of conscience' will be ruled out. Once the mechanisms of the super-ego are exposed as the primitive and often maladaptive processes they are, the enlightened man can no longer be seriously bound by them.

How, then, does the super-ego arise? Freud locates the genesis of morality in the forces of libido and aggression (of love and hate) as they dominate the early life of the child. Morality, he claims, arises with 'the passing of the Oedipus complex'. It is easiest to trace this process in the case of males, though there is a corresponding account, involving the 'Electra complex', of course, for females. All little boys, Freud's account claims, love and desire their mothers. But their fathers prevent them doing anything about it, and so the fathers are hated, as objects of competitive jealousy. The boy wants to kill his father. He cannot do so in fact, and so he kills him symbolically, by the 'introjection' of the father-image into the self. It is as though the father is symbolically killed and eaten. But then, by being devoured, the father goes on living within the self. He becomes a father-image, living in oneself, punishing and repressing. Moreover, this image does not need to correspond to the real father, who may be inoffensive and loving. It takes on the character of the imaginary monster whom the boy hates, as the object of his irrational jealousy. It is this punishing, vindictive, monstrous father-image that is the basis for the super-ego, repressing completely all thoughts of desire for the mother. It also creates a strong sense of anxiety or guilt, at the thought of the imaginary (but psychologically real) killing of this imaginary father, which is at the basis of all the seemingly inexplicable taboos on sex that dominate so much human life. So the rise of morality in the human being lies in the genesis of primitive sexual taboos, sexual guilt and a repressive authoritarian conscience.

Freud says of the genesis of the super-ego: 'When we were little children we knew these higher natures (our parents), we admired them and feared them; and later we took them into ourselves.'[1] The super-ego is the inner representative of our parents, whom we both loved, hated (through frustration of our desires) and feared (because of their superior power, punishing our hatred). But it is not our real parents who are represented, but a set of fantasy images we ourselves had first projected on to them.

So, in the human infant, there is a love that is entirely possessive and centred on libido or sexual pleasure, and causes continual anxiety in case the loved object should be lost. And there is an aggressive hatred, born of frustration, which is projected on to the parents and subsequently introjected again as a cruel and repressive super-ego. Moreover, since the expression of these aggressions is bound to be thwarted by adults and often punished by them, aggression is often redirected against the self. So the mechanism of sado-masochism is created — a seeming need for punishment and a pleasure in being punished.

This syndrome can be perceived in people whom we call 'accident-prone'. They continually put themselves into positions in which accidents occur; thus they satisfy their auto-aggression, and gain a certain power over those others of whom they are really afraid, by drawing sympathy from them.

Suicide can be the final expression of this sado-masochistic complex. But the very conscientious person is exhibiting the same behaviour when he frequently blames himself and feels guilty, and thus exhibits the intropunitive reactions of one who is turning his repressed aggression against himself.

It is in this way that the 'sense of sin' arises for faults for which one feels responsible, even though one can do nothing about them. From this process, too, arises the sense of the absolute necessity of ethical norms. And, in its extreme form, the sense of despair and moral failure that arises from unconscious self-hatred. What the Christian religion had depicted as taking place at the beginning of human history, in the Garden of Eden, Freud plausibly accounts for in terms of the childhood experiences of the individual. But Freud's account is so pessimistic and brutal that morality itself seems to stand revealed as a pathological phenomenon. It does indeed control behaviour, but only by means of deception, lack of awareness and introjected sado-masochism. Naturally enough, religious belief fares even worse, and turns out to be the projection back on to external reality of the punitive father-figure whom we have introjected into ourselves. Conscience is, indeed, the voice of God, for Freud. But both God and conscience are repressive and irrational mechanisms for dealing with infantile emotions and impulses.

If we turn with revulsion from this revelation of the repressive character of religion and morality, we may at least think that there is a more positive side to morality. Is there not also an ego-ideal, which can set the goals and aims a man strives for, and so is positive rather than merely limiting and negative? But there is no escape from Freud's relentless pursuit. The genesis of the ego-ideal is traced to the same primary forces that constitute the inhibiting super-ego.

Freud held that part of the libido, or sexual energy, is narcissistic; that is, it is directed to the self; it forms a sort of sexually based self-love. But, since the real self very often proves to be an unsatisfactory love-object, the child tends to construct an ideal image of the self, to which it then directs its narcissistic libido. This ideal image is made up, primarily, of the introjected approvals and disapprovals of others. At first these others are the parents, but later models may be taken from many diverse sources – stories, plays, society or religion. The function of the ego-ideal is to preserve the self from social pain, in the form of disapproval or rejection. So it basically has the character of a façade, which keeps up socially sanctioned appearances. This façade eventually becomes taken into the self and completely identified with it, causing guilt and anxiety by failure to conform to it.

So the ego-ideal is not formed by some special moral perception or altruistic striving; it is formed by aggressive or narcissistic sexual drives. It is not surprising, then, that a great deal of human misery is caused by a hypertrophied, over-developed, ego-ideal; or by internal conflicts in the ideal, derived from the different models adopted by the ego at various stages of its development.

The psychoanalytical account of morality shows how both ideal-morality and duty-morality, both the positive goals of human striving and the negative, repressive limiting inhibitions on natural instincts and desires, arise in infantile experience out of the interplay of sexual energy and aggression. They grow from the processes of projection and introjection, by means of which the growing child learns to interpret its self and its environment. The super-ego is a complex and unconscious mechanism which functions so as to fit the growing human for social life. On the whole, it performs this function adequately, as one would expect of a mechanism that has enabled the human species to achieve absolute dominance in its habitat. But it does so at great cost to many particular individuals. It could almost be said that the cost of the morality of conscience is widespread neurosis, irrational anxiety and the crippling of many human lives by a morbid sense of guilt. Moreover, with the increasing power brought about by the rise of technology, the destructive effects of repressed aggression and libido – which issue in the need for punishment, and can be satisfied by the vicarious punishment of an 'enemy' onto whom we project our own 'guilt' – the mechanism has itself become hypertrophied and counteradaptive to the further survival of the species.

Freud pointed out that the whole of human culture and civilization is built upon repression of the instincts, and their sublimation to alternative goals of artistic expression or mastery over nature. The basis of culture is unbridled eroticism repressed ruthlessly by inner-directed forces of aggression. Morality and culture thus function as a result of self-destructive tendencies in human nature. As Freud writes, 'The ego is meeting with a fate like that of the protozoa which are destroyed by the products of disintegration that they themselves have created.'[2] The human species has forced itself into a sort of social co-operation by methods of inner disintegration. They may well eventually erupt and complete the process that morality has already begun, totally destroying the organisms that created it. Morality and culture are creations of a being that has to struggle to bring the pleasure-principle (the natural and immediate gratification of impulses, found in the 'id') into uneasy harmony with the reality-principle (by which the ego attains a representation of the environment in its often hostile nature). But they succeed only by creating a destructive potential that could finally eliminate their creator.

Of course the issue is now complicated because the ego has reached the stage of being conscious of the mechanism of the repressing super-ego and the true nature of the id and its natural impulses. So man can discern the power of his impulses of sexual libido and aggression. He can discern the infantile mechanisms of the absolute moral codes imposed by the introjected super-ego. It may seem that there is now a possible escape from the repressive, unwieldy and ultimately self-destructive force of morality. There may be a conscious and rational adjustment of the claims of the id, working in accordance with the pleasure-principle, to the claims of social life and the necessary frustrations it imposes. If most neuroses arise out of an irrationally resolved conflict between id and super-ego, perhaps a rational and conscious resolution of such inevitable conflicts as there are will prevent neuroses and preserve a state of mental health.

So in practice most Freudian analysts find themselves witnessing and tacitly encouraging a process of rejection of super-ego or conscience-morality. They encourage its replacement by the goal of mental health, or psychical adjustment. Just as the biologists have made clear the sub-rational and instinctive bases of the sorts of 'moral' behaviour man as a species shares with many other species of animals, so the psychoanalysts have made clear the sub-rational and repressive psychological forces that give rise to conscience-morality and its seemingly absolute and inescapable constraints. In each case, to understand this is to weaken to some extent the compelling force of those behavioural and psychological constraining factors.

Freud's exposure of the psychological mechanism of conscience-morality does not imply that there will henceforth be no need of super-ego development. Children still have to progress through the long period of infantilism, which is one of the chief distinguishing marks of the human species. The impulses of libido and aggression will still have to be controlled by parental and introjected authorities. So authoritarian morality will remain a necessary phase through which all humans have to pass on their path to maturity, an instrument for shaping children into conformity with their parents' patterns of life and belief. But this view of morality as a training of the infant into social acceptability is very different from the traditional view of man as the uniquely moral animal, who finds his greatest and most mature glory in obedience to the dictates of a duty that transcends his own being. As for the religious enforcements of such traditional moral views, they will inevitably collapse as we come to realize that they are founded on illusions and wish-fulfilment.

Moral training will still be given to children; though, indeed, the moral, in this sense, will be indistinguishable from the permitted and the forbidden. Perhaps it may even prove advantageous to keep most people in this infantile, conditioned state. As the evolutionary moralist Herbert Spencer suggested, the goal of social engineering is to make human beings desire to do what they have to do to fulfil their social function. Whether one does this by genetics, neurosurgery or ideological training, it may well be generally desirable to ensure that people continue to be obedient to the authoritarian morality of their childhood.

But it remains true that to know you have been conditioned is to change your cognitive response to the conditioning process just as to know that a psychologist is manipulating you is bound to affect your response to him. The man who knows himself will see the nature and limits of his 'moral' conditioning. So, little by little, perhaps, where the conditioning is unpleasant or difficult or frustrating, it can be ignored or altered. The Freudian analysis of the super-ego makes it clear that morality, as we know it, is founded on authority, on the unconscious play of instincts in infantile experience. The rational man, armed with this knowledge, though he can never be wholly free of irrational impulses and repressions, will strive to increase his area of consciousness and rationality and thus seek to move beyond morality altogether. What the rational man should aim at is simply reduction of mental conflict, or, more positively, at mental health. The pursuit of morality for its own sake can no longer be considered as a rational goal for men who have attained maturity, who have come of age.

Duty and conscience, then, together with God and the soul, are to be abandoned. But what is to be put in their place? The concept that has appealed to many in the psychoanalytic tradition is that of mental health, or human fulfilment. Erich Fromm sets out the contrast very clearly as one between 'authoritarian ethics' and 'humanistic ethics'. Authoritarian ethics, he says, derives its moral norms from a source outside, and believed to transcend, man. It regards the chief virtue as obedience and the chief vice as disobedience. It is essentially the same as Freud's repressive morality, as the morality of conscience and duty. Humanistic ethics, however, derives from human nature itself. Man is the sole source of ethical norms.

The sole criterion of ethical value is man's welfare. This is a rational morality of self-realization and the fulfilment of your distinctive possibilities.

Fromm asserts that virtue is identical with true self-love. The person who loves himself is truly the productive character, who in his relation to the world and other people realizes all the possibilities of each situation with care, respect, responsibility and knowledge. Evil, on the other hand, is in reality a form of self-hatred or misunderstanding. You adopt a non-productive orientation, and relate to the world and others either by sado-masochistic symbiosis (that is, you seek to devour or be consumed by the other, and so lose yourself in complete identity) or by withdrawal and destructiveness (when you seek to dissociate yourself from or destroy others). This non-productive orientation exemplifies what Freud called the 'pregenital character'. It corresponds to a regression to the oral or anal fixation of libido and a failure to move to a fully genital, productive orientation.

The Freudian analysis is thus used to translate what used to be moral terms into psychological, and supposedly scientific, terminology. We can stop asking what we ought to do, Fromm suggests. That is too misleading and reminds us too much of repressive morality. Instead, we should ask what will make us most mature and healthy. This humanistic ethics is a form of enlightened self-love. It arises from the perception that the self-centred person is 'necessarily unhappy', empty and frustrated – not immoral, but ill. If it seems as though some selfish people are not frustrated and unhappy, Fromm replies that they are unconsciously unhappy; and this can be revealed by analysis. 'Destructiveness is a pathological phenomenon comparable to suicidal impulses . . . the destructive person is unhappy even if he has succeeded in attaining the aims of his destructiveness'.[3] Real happiness can never come from irrational cravings, arising from insecurity, anxiety or greed.

Fromm speaks as if the connection between true self-love and true happiness was established by scientific observation. It seems as though medical science alone can determine that love, security and creativeness are preferable to anxiety, insecurity and greed. But this is a very odd conclusion to draw from Freudian theory. On that theory, man is basically motivated by id-impulses and the function of the ego is to achieve more certain gratification of these. But these impulses – of hunger, sex, fight and flight – may conflict with each other and lead to extreme destructiveness. There is no licence in the Freudian analysis of human nature for talk of a 'true function' of man, which is to live well, or fulfil his possibilities. All man can hope for is to realize as many of his conflicting impulses with as little obstruction and frustration as possible.

It might even be said that Fromm's emphasis on productive possibilities and love and creativeness is just the sort of thing Freudian analysis most clearly reveals as inept, ineffective and impossibly idealistic; just the very prescription, in fact, that causes so much neurosis by its unattainability. Of course, Fromm attempts to deprive the moralizing of its sting by advocating an 'objective', non-judging, attitude towards human behaviour. But the fact remains that people will always fall short of what they pose as the ideal of productive humanity. It is all right to aim at creativeness and love in the abstract. But when it conflicts with your strongest desires here and now, the rational thing to do is to find a more attainable ideal, more suited to man as he actually is. In fact, the most rational thing would be to renounce any human ideal at all, and just get on with pursuing the pleasure-principle to the extent that it is reasonably possible in present social conditions.

Fromm's analysis of human fulfilment and welfare does not seem to be morally neutral at all. It is suspiciously like the traditional Christian view that one supreme moral aim of human life is self-realization, or the use of all the gifts and talents God has given, and the pursuit of final happiness, which Christians say lies in the vision of God. This goal is rooted in human nature, which is created by God for the purpose of achieving self-realization through love and worship and creative activity. For believers, human nature really does have a purpose, which is given to it by God. There is an objective human ideal, not just invented by men, but inherent in their very nature. But Fromm has no right to be talking like that. For him, there is no real purpose in human life; there is no creation and no objective moral goal to be realized. But is he not allowing moral and purposive considerations to enter, unacknowledged, into a supposedly scientific, value-free account of human nature?

Fromm seems to be stuck on the horns of a dilemma. If he is really seeking for a morally neutral account of mental health, he will have to confine himself to such things as mental subnormality and insanity. Even there, we cannot completely escape value terms, but at least you don't get involved in talking about moral goals and ideals. But if he insists on saying that true self-realization lies in the cultivation of responsible love, then he is back into morality in a big way. He is just defining self-realization in the way he wants and he is giving it unmistakable moral overtones. So all this grand talk about humanistic ethics being quite different from authoritarian ethics is very misleading. He *says* he is letting man invent his own moral norms. But he does not let him do so in fact; for if someone chooses a selfish or destructive norm, he just calls it 'pathological', and rules it out by definition. This means that he really does think there are objective standards of human behaviour, and these are rooted in human nature and its purposes. That is just what believers have said all along. So Fromm is indulging in a misleading sort of double-think. He sounds very radical, when he claims that duty and conscience and morality must go. But he brings them all back in again when he talks of man's rational fulfilment and purpose.

However, his account is deficient by comparison with a theistic account, for he seems to let self-realization count as the one supreme value. The trouble with this is brought out very well in the words of Aristotle, who had a similar view: 'He is not at all capable of happiness who is very ugly, or is ill-born or solitary and childless.'[4] The comfortable elitism of moralities of self-realization and happiness is clearly exposed in this remark. Wherever you start talking about self-realization, you are dangerously near a sort of elitism that confines it to the favoured few, and has to condemn the mass of the world's population to a life of misery and conformity. The luxury of self-realization is not for them.

The theistic view is saved from this elitism by its paradoxical insight that true self-fulfilment is found in self-denial, in devotion to God – or, again, remembering the Buddhist alternative, in following the 'Middle Way' to enlightenment. 'True' happiness or self-fulfilment is not as obvious as Fromm seems to think, in other words. It takes spiritual insight to see what it is; and so moral discernment is bound up with insight into what it is to be human, with what it is to be a self, a subject of experience and responsible action. Morality, in other words, is not at all a matter of blind obedience to tyrannical authority. It is a matter of growing discernment into what it means to be human – a discernment deepened and extended, not restricted, by revelation. So we can say that Fromm's protests against authoritarian morality are totally correct. Where he goes wrong is in not realizing his own commitment to a positive and purposive view of human nature, and in not recognizing the deeper insights into what it is to be human, which revelation has provided.

But at least we might say that Fromm has tried to preserve a sort of humanism, a sort of belief in the basic importance of human experience and action. A more ruthlessly consistent application of Freudian ideas to morality would end in the elimination of conscience and duty altogether from the scene. Rejecting the infantile demands of conscience, we might seek a more successful implementation of our own desires. If conscience-morality is decisively rejected, humanistic ethics cannot remain on the agenda. What remains is the will to power and pleasure, released upon the world without any of the traditional moralistic restraints. That is indeed a world we might justifiably fear.

What is the real strength, then, of Freud's attack on duty and conscience? We must first note that it would be silly to judge the normal by the pathological. If Freud has uncovered cases where morality has become diseased, it would be quite wrong to think that all cases of morality were like that. Morality might be better seen by contrast with Freud's cases than by similarity. Furthermore, we must be aware that there is a certain shock effect in Freud's descriptions, which dissipates on closer examination. He tends, for example, to describe all examples of love in terms of sexual attraction, and if you are not aware of any sexual attraction, he can always say that you have repressed the idea, so you can never win. But we can play the opposite game equally well, and suggest that sexual attraction is only a substitute for love, or a primitive form of love, or a desperate attempt to find love. We don't have to fall for the trick of always describing human feelings in their lowest, most animal terms. We may rather choose to see the animal as a proper but limited form of the spiritual desire. Thus sexual activity in human beings is indeed often animal in nature – or rather worse than that, since it is uncontrolled by a season of rut. But we can see that as a pathological condition perverting the real function of human sexuality – namely, to be a physical expression of personal fidelity and commitment. We can say, in other words, that sexuality, in humans, is a limited and often perverse expression of the desire to find or express love. We do not have to say that all human love is just an expression of animal sexuality.

So if the super-ego is seen as a repressive censor, enforcing irrational taboos on sex, we can say that this is part of the pathology of morality, not its normal form. To find that normal form, we do not have to suppose that conscience is the directly known voice of God or that it is infallible – these have never been mainstream theistic beliefs. When a believer speaks of conscience, he is speaking of a rational judgement of value, arising from intelligent reflection on the facts, and from an apprehension of a moral claim. This sense of claim or demand is of the very essence of theistic moral experience; it is indeed part of what a believer means by apprehending the will of God. But it can be mistaken, like any other apprehension or claim to apprehend something. It needs to be rationally checked by thought and careful inspection of available facts. And it must not be confused with a sense of compulsion or neurotic anxiety. In the end, we must do what we believe to be right, but we must be very careful that we have thought hard about it, and investigated all the lines of argument we can discover on the subject.

For example, if we want to come to a moral decision on abortion, it is no use sitting waiting for a sudden command from God, or doing whatever we feel most strongly. We have to study all the facts, examine similar cases, ask where our principles might lead us if we follow them consistently, and see whether there is anything we have failed to take into account. Then we must distinguish what we think is right from what is convenient, or what our parents tell us, or what we might want. In the end, to follow conscience is to think carefully, to seek the fullest sensitivity to all aspects of the issue, and then to do what we believe to be the right thing, whether or not it fulfils us or gives us pleasure. Acting from duty is not following some unreflective impulse, as Freud sometimes suggests. It is acting from the most reflective and rational consideration we can manage.

When Freud talks of the mechanisms of introjection and projection, of our fear and envy of others, he is pointing to enormously important sources of human conduct. He is talking of what Christians have called 'sin', the subterfuges of human self-deception. His analysis here is often excellent and of enduring worth. Where it can go wrong is in suggesting that all conscience-morality is like that; or that guilt is always a form of psychological disease that must be simply removed; or that human ideals are just forms of narcissistic self-love. We do not have to explain the highest human achievements in terms of their primitive origins or their neurotic perversions. Conscience has its part to play, in reminding us that sometimes we should do what is right, simply because it is right. Guilt may come to us because we really have done something terribly wrong, and we must find some way of coping with that fact. Human love and ideals of action can be much more than forms of sexual attraction or social pressure, and it misunderstands human life to reduce them to those less-than-human forces.

In short, psychoanalysis reminds us that we have an animal heritage; that the conscious self is less in control than we sometimes think; and that we do have many impulses in us that derive from infantile formations and experiences. But none of this undermines the truth that there is still a subject of rational consciousness, possessing some degree of responsibility, and able to direct itself in accordance with distinctively moral principles and beliefs. Of course the soul is not a wholly free spiritual subject, able to subdue our impulses consciously and fully. It is a complex interplay of many impulses and desires, not always conscious or controllable. But at its core is a self able to formulate distinctively moral ideas – ideas of actions that should be performed simply because they are right. This is not, in its proper form, the work of a blind, infantile, repressive mechanism, which must be replaced by the acceptance of the pleasure-principle. It is, on the contrary, the activity of the responsible and reflective self, the actual subject of a developing self-awareness and self-control. Its morality is not irrational, but the perfection of reason, as it is applied to perception and action in the world.

We should therefore refuse to accept any contrast between a humanistic morality, supposed to be invented by free decision, and an authoritarian morality, supposed to be given by an unquestionable God or conscience. For we are not free to make up any moral principles we like; we are constrained by reason, by understanding, by sympathy and by the perception of value. Yet that constraint is perceived and accepted only by the fullest use of reason and our highest human faculties. Only when we can speak of conscience, of perception of its demands and acceptance of its claims, can we say that we are truly human. To possess a human soul is to possess the capacity to become fully responsible, by our own choice. We cannot abandon that capacity without losing our proper freedom, which is at the same time our true and rational obedience.

I have defended the idea of the soul against views that seek to see man in a strange and paradoxical way as at the same time free, rational and autonomous, and yet also determined in his behaviour by sub-rational forces which he can do little or nothing to modify or mitigate. There is one more very important strand of modern thought that embodies the same strange ambivalence. It is perhaps the most influential of all, on a world scale, and it sets itself up as an overt competitor with all religious and traditional moral views. It stems from the thought of Karl Marx; and it is to consideration of Marx's thought on these subjects that I now turn.

5

THE MATERIALIST
DENIAL OF THE SOUL

VERY FEW ASPECTS OF modern thought have escaped the influence of Karl Marx. His influence has divided the world into opposing ideological blocs, and some form of his doctrine has been the basis for a system under which millions of people have lived, and in which millions have believed. It may well be that the doctrine is inherently self-destructive, and even that it has already been shown to be so, in the collapse of the Soviet system. Yet Marxists continue to claim that 'true Marxism' has not yet been tried; and it still has a strong intellectual influence, at least in countries that have not suffered from it in practice.

Marx formulated no systematic doctrine himself; his thought is complex, changing and not always influenced by considerations of consistency. There can be no doubt, however, that Marx was deeply opposed to the practice of religion and to the traditional idea of the soul as a self-determining moral subject, called to an eternal destiny and bearing a uniquely valuable inner life. At least in the more systematic works of some of his disciples, he becomes an enemy of the soul. And in his works we can find the same central paradox that is evident in so many attackers of the human soul. On the one hand, a central theme of his work is human freedom and the establishment of a more truly human society, in which creative action and self-realization will be possible for all. On the other hand, he reduces morality to a shadow of the real causal forces of social production and exchange, and makes the whole of human culture and belief dependent upon sub-personal forces that proceed by their own inevitable laws. Of course, he cannot really have both of these things. But such an inconsistency tends to arise when a thinker rejects God, the truly personal basis and origin of human existence, and yet is reluctant to abandon the value of personhood and moral striving altogether. Once the personal basis of existence has gone, we have to account for our existence in terms of sub-personal forces of blind chance or pointless necessity. Then it is virtually impossible to give an absolute value to human life as such, except by an arbitrary decision of will. The tension runs deep, and is very evident throughout Marx's works.

Thus the 'official view' is that, 'in every historical epoch, the prevailing mode of economic production and exchange, and the social organisation necessarily following from it, form the basis upon which is built up, and from which alone can be explained, the political and intellectual history of that epoch'.[1] Social organization 'necessarily follows from' a mode of production and exchange; and it in turn gives rise to the intellectual and moral ideas and beliefs of a given historical period. In the body of the *Communist Manifesto*, the 'bourgeois notions of freedom, culture, law, etc.' are said to be 'but the outgrowth of the conditions of your bourgeois production'. So, for instance, 'the bourgeois family will vanish as a matter of course when its complement (private gain) vanishes'.[2] Again, 'law, morality, religion, are to him (the proletarian) so many bourgeois prejudices'.[3] For 'man's ideas, views and conceptions, in one word, man's consciousness, changes with every change in the conditions of his material existence'; so that 'the ruling ideas of each age have ever been the ideas of its ruling class'.[4] The whole of social history has been a history of class struggle, and the morality of private property and family reflect the social dominance of the superior class. However, Marx predicted that, with the rise of the proletariat, the last class barriers would be overthrown. When the workers, the poorest class, are liberated from oppression, there will be no further inferior class to liberate. Thus the classless communist society will be ushered in by the proletarian revolution. Private property and the bourgeois family would disappear, with all their accompanying moral values.

Marxism is as complex a system of ideas as is any religion; so there are a number of possible interpretations and developments of Marx's thought. He himself was an economic historian, more concerned about his analysis of conditions in late nineteenth-century Britain than with exact predictions about the far communist future. Nevertheless, it is a central theme of his thought to say that all moral, political and religious values are governed by social structures, by structures of production and exchange, not by individual ideas or abstract theorizing. He is not saying that there are no moral values. He is saying that moral values depend upon primarily economic relations and that the moral values of the bourgeoisie, which are based on the preservation of private property, implicitly regarding women and children as pieces of property, too, will inevitably disappear as the privileged and propertied class inevitably disappears.

It is also a central Marxist thesis that there is a virtually inevitable law of historical development, by which one social phase of existence passes over into another. Marx's view is meant to be a strictly *scientific* materialism, not a mere philosophical theory. Once again, we have the Enlightenment appeal to 'science' as the arbiter of truth and the ultimate authority for morality. It is said to be a matter of scientific fact that history can be seen to be moving in a specific direction. History progresses dialectically – that is, from one social condition (say, feudalism) to its opposite (capitalism) and then to a higher synthesis (in this case, socialism). That synthesis in turn becomes the thesis of a new spiral in the dialectical progress. At least, this should happen in principle, but Marx speaks as though the dialectical progression would end with the final foundation of a classless society. He had an extremely vague idea of what such a society would be like, and one of the main problems of Marxist-inspired revolutions is that there is no clear programme of how to get from the transitional dictatorship of the proletariat to the goal of the classless society, when dictatorship would wither away. Still, it is an essential part of the theory that history has a definite goal, to which it is inevitably progressing.

This goal is sketched out, particularly in some of Marx's early writings, as a society in which every individual would be able freely to express his or her own nature creatively. There would be no coercion, no oppression, no compulsion. All would give what they could and take what they needed.[5] Freedom and self-realization would be possible for all, and not just for one small dominant class. The echoes of the Kingdom of God are unmistakable; and it is no coincidence that Marx was born a Jew and baptized a Christian as a baby. The great difference, of course, is that there is no God in this Kingdom. But otherwise it is the Kingdom of peace and plenty, the society of abundance, of which the Bible so often speaks.

Even the absence of God is rather ambiguous. There is certainly no personal being to whom one can relate in love and devotion. But in a strange way, although the dialectic of history is materialistic (that is, it is founded not on any spiritual reality, but on economic forces and social forms of activity), it is also purposive. The scientific examination of historical change can show that history has a goal, and this is a moral goal, which it is the duty of each person now living to help bring about. Marx believed strongly in the primacy of action over theory, and his calls to unite against oppression and strive for justice are unmistakably moralistic in tone. The driving force of Marxism is a burning sense of injustice and the desire for a more just society. So it seems that history is inevitably moving towards a moral goal.

The thought of Marx is deeply influenced by Hegel, who first fully developed the view of history as exemplifying an evolutionary progress towards the full self-expression of

Absolute Spirit. In Hegel's view, it is (more or less) intelligible that the course of history should be both purposive and morally orientated, because its ultimate foundation is a completely coherent, rational and conscious spiritual reality, which Hegel calls *Geist* or Absolute Spirit. But Marx said that he had found Hegel's system and stood it on its head. That is, he made the reality, of which history is a temporal appearance, not spirit, but matter, a non-conscious, unthinking, unfeeling process. But how can this unthinking, sub-personal reality be thought of as having a moral purpose?

I think the blunt answer is that it cannot. Marx is trying to keep his cake and eat it. He is trying to get rid of a personal, providential God, who has a moral purpose in making the world. But he is also trying to keep talking about the world as though it has an inevitable moral purpose. The consequence is that he talks of a sort of 'de-personalized' purpose, a sort of 'de-idealized' morality, and a sort of 'dehumanized' idea of personal dignity and worth.

So at times he talks as though all human feelings, all efforts and action, all systems of human thought, from mathematics to poetry and philosophy, every belief and attitude, are caused by historical and economic processes of which men are largely unconscious. Yet at other times he speaks movingly of the obligation to actualize human freedom, to make the world more human and to take responsibility for the future. Sometimes he talks as if all moral systems are merely rationalizations of self-interest — the ideology of the ruling class. But at other times he seems to envisage a possible society in which self-interest will have disappeared, and people will be able to co-operate productively and creatively. Sometimes he speaks as if our own moral views are determined by our own society; as if they will change as society changes; and as if no view is really better or worse than any other. But at other times he speaks as if it is obvious to all right-thinking people that a classless society without oppression is objectively and absolutely better than a society in which oppression and exploitation exist.

Now these ambiguities are important, and they point to a deep flaw in Marx's idea of the human soul, of human nature, of what it is to be a human person. The flaw is that Marx's whole philosophical approach is devoted to undermining the idea of spiritual realities and their agency; it is a form of materialism. And yet he cannot really face the implications of materialism, when it comes to the point. So he tries to stress the importance of human freedom and action – in fact, of just those spiritual activities of knowledge, creativity and love that believers find so important. Yet because in the end he thinks that history is driven by sub-personal forces, his ideas of human freedom and rationality and morality become seriously compromised.

The parallels with biblical, and especially with Old Testament, morality, are clear. History has a moral goal; one people, or section of the world's population, are marked out to realize this goal. There is an absolute demand for justice in society. There is a clear perception of the dignity of labour (unlike Greek philosophy, which saw no point in work at all). There is an inevitable historical judgement on oppressors and exploiters of the poor. Marx's searing indictments of social injustice are very near in tone to the denunciations of the Old Testament prophets who consistently supported the poor and oppressed against the rich and militaristic.[6]

But in the Bible it is God who gives history its purpose; God who chooses people to do his will; God who demands justice and who gives dignity to labour; and God who judges oppressors and hypocrites. What has Marx to put in place of God? He has to place his faith in the material dialectic of history itself, and this fatally infects his understanding of morality. Because of his materialism, he makes moral ideas epiphenomenal upon economic processes. So he is unable to advocate the pursuit of reason, truth and goodness for their own sakes. Rather, these things are the by-products of particular sets of social relations. This leads to a cynicism about the importance of freedom of investigation and criticism, to censorship and a closed ideology. If all truth and morality follow from material circumstances, then we will not pursue truth for itself; we will change the material situations, and changes of belief will follow. But how are we to change those situations? Without rational guidance, we will simply have to say that they change inevitably, by the inner momentum of their own historical laws. But in this way we have reduced morality to an outgrowth of economics, that is, to a matter of technique and manipulation. We no longer have any standards by which to judge our own society.

There is a certain irony about Marx's position at this point. For it looks as if his view can lead to extreme conservatism as well as revolutionary fervour. Indeed, it will almost inevitably become a very conservative view, in the end. Marx felt justified in advocating the overthrow of capitalist society, because he felt it was historically doomed – and he pronounced that doom as a result of a 'scientific' study of history. But if, as he says, moral views are moulded by social structures, it is equally reasonable to think that loyalty to your present society, to the status quo, should be a basic moral principle. After all, if you think that society is the source of your moral opinions, it is a short step to say that society is always more right than the individual, so that you should accept the current social morality and not attempt to revise it.

Now the actual progress of Marxism, as a political ideology, seems to illustrate this trend; for in Marxist societies, criticism of the existing (Marxist) ideology is strongly discouraged, and individual moral belief is subordinated entirely to the socially accepted creed. The revolutionary creed has become a conservative dogma. Moreover, it is impossible to reject this view on moral grounds; because morality, on the theory, is the expression of social structure. If moral beliefs are seen to be simply results of social conditioning, we can no longer accept morality as an absolute and overriding normative code. But then, we cannot help coming to realize that our own social conditioning is not of decisive importance or unchangeable validity either. As the social anthropologist Ruth Benedict writes of eighteenth-century New England, 'we are faced with the fact that the group of people who carried out to the greatest extreme and in the fullest honour the cultural doctrine of the moment are by the slightly altered standards of our generation the victims of intolerable aberrations'.[7] The implication is that we should be careful, if we are rational, not to take our own cultural codes too seriously. We must then, it seems, be sceptical conservatives – we will follow custom and convention, but with a certain ironic detachment, realizing that we follow only one way among many, and that there is really no 'better' or 'worse'.

But now this is as far as we could possibly get from the view that the one finally serious business of life is to discover what it is to be just and moral, or to pursue virtue with passionate inwardness. The final impact of the Marxist interpretation of morality is decisively to overthrow the traditional morality both in its Judaeo-Christian form and in its reinterpretation in terms of an evolutionary purposive goal in orthodox Marxist theory. When we see what, on this account, morality is, we simply cannot any longer take it too seriously. The revolutionary fervour that is founded on the perception of injustice and is so much part of the attraction of Marxism, evaporates into the sceptical conservatism of a way of life that sees itself to be rationally unjustifiable, but a more or less inevitable by-product of a certain social structure. It is only the absolute moral demands of a God who transcends all human societies that can deliver one from such sceptical relativism. In a strange way, Marx has cut off the very roots from which his own thought grew, and which alone could support it and deliver it from cynicism.

There is another central feature of Marx's thought that results in moral ambiguity. It might well be called the distinctive contribution of Marxist thinking to the modern western view of human nature. It is the emphasis on the social character of the individual; the socially conditioned character of the individual's beliefs, hopes, dreams and fears. 'The real nature of man', says Marx, 'is the totality of social relations.'[8]

Since the ascendancy of Christianity, the West has advocated the cult of the individual. Though for many centuries the Church in a sense subordinated individual judgement to its own hierarchic teaching authority, the faith it preserved unequivocally made the individual and his eternal destiny the most important features of the human situation. At the Reformation, this stress on the importance of the individual was made even more marked by the emergence of a doctrine of individual guidance by conscience, as enlightened by the devout reading of Scripture. As the Age of Enlightenment progressed, Scripture too was left behind, and the reason and conscience of each person became his final and sufficient guide. Thus, in the early years of the scientific revolution, most thinkers automatically conceived of man atomistically, as a discrete individual who entered only contingently into relations with his fellows. Though religious inspiration was soon dropped from these schemes, the motivating forces of human conduct continued to be internal to the individual, the force of individual pleasure and pain taking the place of the 'inner light'. It is typical of the political theorists of the sixteenth to eighteenth centuries to speak of society as formed by mutual agreement to a social contract, a restriction of liberty in order to secure peace and stability. Man in the 'state of nature' was rarely conceived as an essentially social animal, and society was commonly conceived as an imposition or restriction on his natural liberty and desires.

Though Marx was by no means the first theorist to reject this atomistic doctrine of human nature, his name and influence is the one that has come to stand for the social approach to human nature. It is typical of the social approach that it denies that man can be understood adequately by just looking at the state of his individual mind. Human beliefs and feelings are socially conditioned and we can only understand them by looking at the social forces that condition them.

Individualist philosophers have always retained, as their paradigm of the self, something like the religious notion of the soul, the inner core of unique, private identity that no one else could ever penetrate, and which endures through all its bodily experiences, and perhaps beyond. The notion of a social self enables us to dispense with this paradigm. In fact, we can even say that the concept of an individual, morally responsible self has arisen through the peculiar type of conditioning that has evolved in western capitalist culture. As Marx puts it, 'the idea of freedom of conscience merely gave expression to the sway of free competition'.[9] It arises from an economic system requiring initiative and free trade.

Many social anthropologists would agree that the self has an essentially social character; that it is a function of its social roles in a given culture. The old atomistic picture of each person as a distinct spiritual being is rejected. Instead, it is said that a personality only comes into being as a result of social interaction. Ashley Montagu writes that a creature apart from a social group is nothing but an organic being, the member of a social group is a person.[10] Talcott Parsons, the influential sociologist, saw society as a series of statuses, or roles, to each of which there is assigned a specific set of rights and duties and a certain prestige. When an individual accepts such a role, he thereby conforms to a relatively stable pattern of reactions and expectations.[11]

Each person can have many roles, but these roles are rather like the successive layers of an onion — when they are all peeled away, there is nothing left. There is no spiritual inner core, which remains when all the roles have been discarded, a 'real self'. It is social institutions that define roles, and we become persons by learning to fulfil such roles — only by the grace of society and the roles it makes available. It is in response to the approvals and disapprovals of others that we develop an image of ourselves. So the truth is the opposite of the old philosopher's picture of each person having primary and privileged access to his own private self. The self is the last thing you come to know, and you know it through the reactions of others.

On this view, morality is built into the structure of roles and their interrelation. It is as if, to use Talcott Parsons' image, each society played a special game. The rules of each game might be different, but each game needs some rules, and some system of penalties for rule-breakers. This is the basis of our moral codes. Each society will need some moral code, but that code may vary widely from one society to another.

In this respect, some of the most interesting and entertaining data have resulted from the work of Margaret Mead and Ruth Benedict, American anthropologists. Benedict traces three main patterns of culture, which, she claims, result from various systems of personality-formation in society.[12] One pattern, which she terms the Apollonian, is exemplified by the Zuni Indians and by the Arapesh, whom Mead investigated. Such people are gentle and easy-going; violence of all kinds is frowned on; those members of the tribe who are violent are regarded as unbalanced, neurotic and are liable to be frustrated and unhappy. Another pattern she calls the Dionysian is a much more extroverted pattern. The Kwakiutl, investigated by Boas, and the Manus, studied by Mead, are given as instances of this pattern. In their culture, there is a cult of conspicuous waste, and there is much competition, fight for status and stress on initiative and drive. A person who would integrate ideally into Arapesh society would find himself a social outcast and 'mentally unhealthy' in Kwakiutl culture, where the ideal approaches what, in most western societies, we would call paranoia. Thirdly, Benedict instances the Dobu of the South Sea Islands, which, if her account is to be believed, is one of the most unpleasant cultures ever studied. The ideal character there is the successful cheat, who has hated, murdered and lied his way to success. No one is trusted and fierceness and competition are the accepted values. Dobu society might almost have been designed as an experimental disproof of the social contract view that small societies must be founded on mutual trust to survive. Mutual hatred seems to serve the same function in Dobu society, and the trusting person is a neurotic fool in that society.

Benedict explicitly draws the moral that the values of a given society are culture-relative; that cultures express projections of favoured personality-formations; and that moral training is a process of conditioning to a culture-pattern. The force of social disapproval is sufficient, in these societies, to induce conformity, suicide or intense unhappiness. Thus, says Benedict, we must accept as 'co-existing and equally valid, patterns of life which mankind has created for itself from the raw materials of existence'.[13]

Marx and Engels drew upon the work of some of the early anthropologists in formulating their view of the correlation between moral norms and the structure of a society. It was perhaps such work that led Marx to suppose the self to be socially conditioned, and that different stages of social organization would lead to different roles, moral norms and ideals for their individual members. But, just as he was not able to accept that we were totally determined by the processes of history, and called us to accept our freedom and responsibility for the future, so he could not really accept that we are nothing but the sum of our social relationships. And he looked for an ideal society in which the State would wither away, and people would be free to organize their own lives without being constricted by imposed roles or alien expectations. But again, one half of his theory exercises a malign influence on the other. Because, at all present stages of history, individuals are constituted by their roles in oppressive social structures, there is a tendency to lose sight of that great inheritance bequeathed by Judaism and Christianity to the modern West – the unique dignity and irreplaceability of each human individual.

In the religious view, every human being is irreplaceable and of quite unique value. The existence of each person has an importance, a meaning and purpose, that cannot be removed. Each person, in the recesses of his own being, remains free in spirit and in his inner response to the call of the supreme spiritual goal. Marx is so conscious of the way in which such a belief can be used to excuse inhumanity and oppression (by saying that people are still 'really' free even when we enslave them), that he tends to deny it altogether. Then freedom consists only in the external freedom to do as one wills, and all the emphasis is put on changing social structures, to the neglect of inner spiritual needs. In the end, we can change the social structures at the expense of individuals. Indeed, whole classes of individuals need to be removed in order to bring about such changes. And thereby is bred a terrible indifference to the fate of individuals, their reduction to the status of means to accomplish a social change, to effect some future hope in which they cannot share.

Because of his emphasis on the social nature of personhood, Marx loses the idea of the dignity of the individual, a dignity that places a limit on any programme of social change. Thus individuals and their own choices become subordinated to State action, to the tyranny of the group over private opinion. Where persons are the sum of their social relationships, and where the structure of social relations is destined to be overthrown by the processes of history, then persons must be treated simply as parts of those doomed processes. Individualism becomes a crime; the structure comes before the value of individual experience; people can be manipulated by centralized planning, so as to bring about some long-term desired goal.

In consequence, this goal – of the classless, completely non-oppressive society – itself becomes Utopian. That is, it becomes impossible to realize in history, because the very means taken to realize it prevent it ever occurring. The Marxist goal is a society of free self-realizing persons. But to realize this goal whole structures of society have to be swept away, whole classes of people – capitalists and bourgeoisie – have to be eliminated, class-conflict has to reach a fever pitch of intensity, ending in violent overthrow of the system. In this way hatred, malice and conflict are built into the system as essential elements – a hatred directed against whole classes, which prevents us from sympathizing with individuals themselves. Through such class-hatred and the contempt for the individual that it breeds, there can never emerge a humane and tolerant and harmonious society. The victorious proletariat will always have to suppress those forces of reaction that threaten to emerge again. The dictatorship of the proletariat, founded on fear and violence, will prove an immovable obstacle to the withering away of a centralized State.

So the sort of morality Marx suggests is a strange mixture of idealism and dehumanizing social engineering. This is fundamentally because his view vacillates between being a complete rejection of morality, in the name of an alleged objective science of history, and a reinterpretation of traditional morality in terms of an inevitable moral goal in history. He talks of purpose, but rejects any notion of a conscious Mind that could be directing it. He talks of morality, but claims that all moralities are disguised expressions of dominant class-relations. He talks of personal freedom, but regards persons as essentially defined by sets of roles in social institutions, by their class-position and economic status. These ambiguities make it fundamentally unclear whether Marxism is a doctrine appealing to a higher morality of justice and equality, or one that overthrows morality altogether, as a bourgeois or class-based self-deception. That lack of clarity renders Marxism a prey to internal forces of tyranny and oppression, which can speak the words of moralism while knowing that their content is in the end empty.

The ambiguities in Marx provide the best critique of his own thought, for they show the points at which belief in the human soul, its moral calling and its irreplaceable dignity, is both important and threatened. I will briefly attempt to summarize the points I have made about the Marxist attack on the soul and its failure.

First, there is the view that all intellectual and moral ideas are determined by social conditions, and are relative to class and culture. This is yet another form of the reductionism with which we are by now familiar. It seems that each scientist is tempted to reduce human life to his own preferred discipline, and this time sociology or economics replaces biology as the favoured 'science'. In addition to the usual caution about confining one's scientific findings to their proper field, and not trying to extend them to cover the whole of experience, there are special problems about seeing sociology, economics or history as 'sciences' in the full sense. Marx's own predictions were notoriously incorrect – he thought revolution would come in England or Germany, but never in Russia. And it hardly seems possible to get reliable predictions of human behaviour at all, except in the most general terms (for example, that people will be pretty selfish much of the time).

It is highly illuminating to consider theories in their social context, to look for social conditions that may have motivated or prompted them. But to hold that some study of economic structures could 'explain', for example, the theory of relativity, seems to miss the point about what relativity is. It may be interesting to know that Einstein had indigestion, and so worked late one night and discovered the theory, but it hardly explains the elegance or truth or plausibility of the theory at all. The human soul has a power of freedom, imagination, discovery and invention, which is not bounded by exact predictions – if it were, no really new discoveries could ever be made, since, to be predictable, they would have to have happened before. And while the soul is obviously born into specific cultures, just as it has a specific genetic character, it has a freedom to shape and transcend those elements, not to be wholly bound by them, but at least partially to direct and shape them. Marx shows the social context of the soul, but he cannot eliminate its ultimate individuality and freedom, its power to transcend social conditions, even the most restricting, in its internal life.

Second, there is not only the attempt to reduce the soul to a material/social process; there is also the attempt to make moral and religious beliefs wholly relative to specific social conditions. When this is perceived, they are bound to seem less important, less worthy of our whole-hearted commitment. But moral relativism is very implausible. As Professor H. L. A. Hart points out, in *The Concept of Law*,[14] people are everywhere bound by certain physiological and environmental factors, which are similar throughout the species. For instance, all people are prone to accident, disease and death. They rely for their preservation on a certain degree of limited affection. They are subject to instincts of hunger, sex, aggression and fear. And they usually have to compete for the use of limited resources. Given the similarity of these factors over virtually all the human species, there will naturally arise certain basic moral principles common to all. Rules like 'Do not kill', 'Do not steal' and so on do not need any special Divine revelation. They are rules which, in general, will exist in all cultures – even the Dobu have some limitations on these activities – as a condition of any sort of social life.

Now this will hardly be enough to inspire moral vision or firm moral commitment. But it does mean that morality is not wholly relative; there are fundamental, quite natural principles of morality, common to all human societies. Reason can establish what these are, and it can go on to assess various social norms in the light of their suitability for achieving human goals. Of course, reason is not infallible, and it does have to start with some specific social situation. But it is able to reflect and assess continually, seeking a more impartial, informed and extensive view. In other words, our beliefs are not solely bound by social conditioning. We can reflect critically, and such reflection may carry us beyond both cultural short-sightedness and cynicism to a stage where we see that there are moral absolutes like truth, love and justice, and that a commitment to these transcends a mere acceptance of our own societies' conventions. It is of basic importance to distinguish our moral beliefs from social conventions. Marx, of course, sees this, but he does not see that his own account of morality as socially relative prevents him from making the distinction in a correct way. Marx sees how moral words may be used as a cloak for self-interest, but he never gives due recognition to the way in which moral values continually challenge our self-interest and hypocrisy, calling the individual soul to a recognition of its true destiny in transcendence of self-interest, to become a truly free moral subject.

Third, there is the attempt to see persons as simply the sum of their social roles. But again, he himself sees that persons can, at least potentially, transcend all imposed roles to become freely self-realizing individuals. His mistake is to postpone to some far Utopian future something that is true here and now. The whole point of talking of the soul is to remind ourselves constantly that we transcend all the conditions of our material existence; that we are always more than the sum of our chemicals, our electrons, our social roles or our genes. We do not transcend them by having an additional, spiritual bit that we can pin down and define. We transcend them precisely in being indefinable, always more than can be seen or described, subjects of experience and action, unique and irreplaceable. It is ironic that Marx sometimes accuses Christianity of under-valuing human dignity now, and postponing it to heaven. For the importance of believing in the soul is that we cannot postpone human dignity at all; it places a limit on all our actions. We can never see someone as just a capitalist or a pro-letarian, a black or a white person. Each person is precious and unique, and should not be treated just as a member of a class. Marx usefully stresses the ways in which persons are essentially social beings, but he fails to stress that, in their individuality, they transcend any social description, and in their dignity they transcend any market value.

Fourth, there is the attempt to have purpose without a purposer, a moral goal without God. It is here that we see one of the most determined efforts in the history of philosophy to eliminate the idea of spiritual transcendence from our view of the world. And it is here that we see how belief in the soul is related to belief in God. For, in a strictly materialist view, the soul can have no place. All the real causal forces of nature are material; there are no spiritual subjects of action, intending to realize ideal states. The essence of spiritual action is that it is free, creative realization of unique and imaginative forms of being. By contrast, material 'actions' are wholly law-governed, determined, repetitive, unconscious and unappreciated processes. The retention of purpose, in a materialist view, is anachronistic, a remnant of a discarded theory. But if it really goes, then there is no place in the world for the unique, the free, the creative and the consciously valued. On the other hand, if those things are seen as real and basic constituents of our world, then we must talk of the actions of free spirits, and in the reality of the human soul the theist sees a faint image of the purely spiritual activity of God, who gives the world a real purpose and moral goal.

Marx was opposed to the idea of the human soul, but that was because he thought the soul was some sort of abstraction, a denial of the body and its needs, a retreat from the hardships of social life into some supposed dream-land of the inner life. The soul, however, is not the negation of the material and the social; it is not some inner world where we can be safe from social conflict. The soul is precisely the activity of the spiritual subject as a real agency within the social and material world. It is only because it has such an agency that it can be responsible for the future and for its world, and that it can hope for the transformation of the material world into a realm of freedom and self-realization for all. The denial of the soul leads to loss of the ideal of individual worth; to loss of a sense of the absolute claims of love and truth; to loss of a real sense of moral purpose and the importance of moral striving in the world. If we are really to seek for justice and human freedom and self-realization for all, it is vital to recognize the human soul for what it is – the transcendent subject that is never wholly bound by the material forms in which it is, nevertheless, truly incarnate. It is because Marx could not see this that his philosophy is capable of leading to hatred, tyranny and oppression – the very things against which he also wanted to fight. The paradox of Marx's view here is just one more example of that modern movement of thought since Nietzsche, which claims to liberate humanity from old ideological oppression, but only succeeds in enslaving it to forces more blind and purposeless. The remedy is not to return to the rule of an old tyrant, but to see that the tyranny was in ourselves, and that the God who is the spirit of compassion and love is a God who gives us, and requires of us, freedom and the awesome power of self-determination in relation to absolute standards of moral goodness.

6

THE ATTACK
ON MORAL OBLIGATION

I HAVE TRACED SOME of the main currents of modern western thought that have led to a cumulative attack on the existence of the soul, on absolute moral standards and on God. The great seminal figures of this movement of thought were all nineteenth-century thinkers whose originality and genius exercised a lasting influence on human ideas. It is only in the work of some of their twentieth-century disciples, however, that the point of their attack has been sharpened and extended to cover the whole range of human activity and thought. What has been constructed out of their thought has been a dominant world view of great seduction and power, a view that may be termed 'scientific objectivism'. The term is rather ironic, for I think the view is neither very scientific nor very objective. But it is meant to point to the basic belief that the whole truth about human nature and the world can be given by the experimental sciences, which are 'objective' in Monod's sense of excluding all considerations of purpose and value. It would, of course, be rather odd if a method of investigation that consciously excluded such very important things could indeed provide the whole truth about a world in which they play such a very conspicuous part. Nevertheless, all such considerations are relegated to the realm of the private and subjective, which is itself an epiphenomenon, a by-product, of material process in the brain, which can be studied in the proper scientific way.

The beginning and necessary basis for scientific objectivism was given by Nietzsche's momentous declaration of the death of God. The elimination of a spiritual basis from reality at a stroke eliminated purpose and value from objective reality. In Nietzsche's eyes, it also freed man from the oppressive tyranny of a monstrous God who required total and unquestioning obedience from his servile subjects. It left man free to create his own moral values, to take control of his own destiny, to achieve true self-mastery. However, the question that remains is whether this liberation from God and from morality, the bold acceptance that there is no purpose or value which we do not ourselves invent or impose on the world, will not lead to an eventual cynical helplessness in the face of the sub-personal drives of passion and impulse which are the only real causes of change in the world and in ourselves. Where there are no moral constraints or ideals, passion may drive us where it will, unguided and uncaring. So, in Nietzsche, we discern already a tension or ambiguity that permeates scientific objectivism – the tension between an apparently ineradicable wish for human freedom and rational morality, and the realization that human action is determined by sub-personal forces that we can do little or nothing to moderate or control.

This 'realization' is, of course, itself a theory that is not, in fact, securely based on the scientific evidence to which it usually appeals. Darwin's epoch-making theory of natural selection has been broadened by some geneticists, molecular biologists and ethologists into a general theory that homo sapiens is an accidental result of random mutation, without purpose or any unique significance in nature. Morality is only a mechanism that has been conducive to the survival of certain genetic codes – and incidentally, as it were, to the survival of our species. When we see this, morality, as anything like a set of absolute constraints, will disappear just as surely as religion will, when we see that it is a similar behaviour-controlling invention.

Nevertheless, the very people who propound this theory are constantly appealing to us to accept it precisely because it is reasonable and true, and to construct a 'fairer' and less irrational or infantile morality and world-view as a result of our knowledge of this truth. They thus appeal to man's unique ability to apprehend truth, to exercise reason, and to act on rational and disinterested principles – the very things the theory reduces to nothing but mechanisms of biological imprinting.

To believe in the soul is to believe that man is not just an object, to be studied, experimented upon and scientifically defined and analysed, manipulated or controlled. It is to believe that man is essentially a subject, a centre of consciousness and reason, who transcends all objective analysis, who is always more than can be scientifically defined, predicted or controlled. In his essential subjectivity, man is a subject who has the capacity to be free and responsible – to be guided by moral claims, to determine his own nature by his response to these claims. He can either grow in sensitivity, wisdom and disinterestedness, or he can refuse to do so, and allow himself to be ruled by the drives for power and pleasure. Even that is his free choice, and the absoluteness of the moral claim lies in the fact that it requires commitment to truth, to reason, to justice, disinterestedness and creativity, simply for their own sakes, and not for any pleasure or benefit they may bring to ourselves or to others.

I have spoken in terms of God, for that is the idea that has been attacked by modern atheists. But non-theistic forms of religion, too, share with religious views in general a belief in the spiritual nature of human beings and in the existence of an objective value and a goal of human striving. In Buddhist terms, the moral law is laid down in the structure of the universe as the law of *karma*. Good and evil actions carry their inevitable consequences for the agent; and release from passion and suffering is only achieved when selfish desire is overcome and *nirvana*, a state of supreme bliss and consciousness, is attained. In such a religious view, there is no God who is an objective commander of the moral law. But the moral law is objective, and it is necessary to follow it to achieve the supreme goal of human life. Where a theist defends God as the basis of morality, a Buddhist would speak rather of the nature of the world as a realm of suffering and the necessity of following the eightfold path to enlightenment. There is a spiritual and objective basis to morality, and that is what is important. If that is rejected, then moral claims lose their absoluteness, the purpose of moral striving disappears and the unique nature of the soul is threatened by the apparently hostile, alien and irrational universe within which it seems to exist. In the world-view of scientific objectivism, there is simply no place for souls, for such mysterious and indefinable things as 'subjects'. All must be reduced to the status of an object, and all must be explained in terms of general laws and causal mechanisms alone.

In fact, such a programme cannot be consistently carried through. The deep inadequacy of materialist views is shown in the fact that they cannot even be seriously stated without compromising their own premises. They inevitably appeal to reason and truth, and to our ability to apprehend such things and adjust our beliefs accordingly. Thus they transcend their own theories, for the adjustment of belief as a result of conscious apprehension and rational reflection is something that cannot be explained in terms of purely causal mechanisms or general laws, which can only deal with repetitive regularities and measurable, publicly observable data.

Accordingly, the strongest criticism of scientific objectivism is that it rests on a fundamental misunderstanding of scientific activity. Science, properly speaking, does not attempt to provide the whole truth about everything. Particular sciences deal with abstract models for measurable and repeatable phenomena. In so far as events in the real world are concrete, non-measurable, new, not publicly observable, not precisely definable or truly intentional, they cannot be enshrined in scientific models, as they are understood at the present time. So, while science can help enormously in building up an accurate picture of the world, it never could provide a total or complete account of how the world is. And working scientists are perfectly aware of that when they leave their laboratories and go home for the evening, into the 'real world' again.

But not only is science unable to account completely for what the world is like. It is also not the impartial, value-free enquiry that scientific objectivists often make it out to be. Scientific enquiry is, on the contrary, a value-laden enterprise. Above all, it is committed very fundamentally to the values of impartiality; disinterested pursuit of truth, wherever it leads; rationality; as well as to such semi-aesthetic values as elegance, beauty, symmetry, simplicity, consistency and coherence. To give people a good training in some scientific discipline is to train them in certain great moral goods. It is to train them in concern for truth, and thus in honesty. It is to train them in impartial investigation, and thus in elementary justice. It is to train them in co-operation and trust within the scientific community, and thus in integrity and understanding. It is to train them in respect for the facts, in the love of intellectual beauty and in a certain sort of self-discipline and self-renunciation, which all good scientific work requires. It is not surprising that scientific objectivists cannot get rid of morality, for they have been trained in disciplines that are deeply and ineradicably moral and founded upon the absolutes of truth, reason and understanding.

The paradox is that such a deeply moral understanding should have given rise to the apparent denial of the uniqueness of the human soul and of the moral absolutes in pursuit of which it finds its proper fulfilment. The real puzzle is to see why this should ever have been so. It seems that somehow, in their minds, morality has got disconnected from truth, and an over-enthusiasm for certain sorts of understanding, which science gives, has rendered them blind to any other sorts of understanding, such as the understanding of the human self, its action and its responsibility. Perhaps the very simplicity, apparent elegance and potential explanatory power of materialism, and the way in which the abandonment of purposive explanations has led to undoubted advances in the sciences, has had a dazzling effect, which has blinded them to some of the very features they deploy in their own theories.

But when such powerful and sensitive minds reject God and morality, they are not reacting against nothing. When Freud rejects conscience-morality and Fromm rejects authoritarian ethics, they are reacting against elements of religion and traditional morality which have been dangerous and damaging, both to individuals and to societies. They are reacting against views that threaten to subordinate man's rational nature to infantile, authoritarian and purely repressive beliefs. They are wanting to insist that morality is not just a matter of parental or social control; that it is a matter of rational judgement and of individual responsibility. The irony is, again, that what they propose has led to a reinstatement, in a different form, of what they feared.

For they leave a view of the human mind as a sort of battle-ground of diverse and conflicting impulses, and they often advocate a rejection of talk about 'duty' in favour of asking 'what you really want, in the long run'. They leave little reason for thinking that there is a possible fulfilment for each human life, and much reason for thinking that the most we can hope for is not to be overwhelmed by our neuroses. The soul is downgraded to a seeker after perpetual pleasure, and morality is down-graded to a mechanism for making our pleasure expectations more realistic. So their final view may not be authoritarian, in the old sense. But it is a view that subordinates the free, rational activity of a moral subject of consciousness to the morally criterionless choice of a bundle of conflicting drives and impulses. Once more, when the soul disappears, morality is compromised; it loses any sense of absoluteness – indeed, such a notion comes to seem absurd or even pathological. And in the end, replaced by the idea of 'mental health', it becomes a means to achieving whatever realistic set of desires one may happen to have, however one came to have them.

The Marxist stress on individual life as part of a socially conditioned reality completes this account by giving those desires in turn a social explanation. Thus the individual is no longer credited with a unique dignity and permitted an area of responsible freedom. Rather, he becomes simply the locus of certain institutionalized roles, a member of a class, and can be treated and manipulated as such. Of course, this is far from the intention of Marx. But that illustrates my main point, which is that scientific objectivism carries within it internal contradictions, which lead it to results that undermine its own deepest intentions.

Thus what Marx most desires is the complete freedom of each individual to realize his or her own creative nature, and thereby to realize the inner goal and purpose of nature. But his own brand of scientific materialism requires him to deny that nature has any purpose; to assert that all systems of moral ideas are rationalizations of class-position; and to deny that individuals are anything more than their socially determined roles. Morality is still primarily (where it is rational at all) the means to realizing desires, and desires are produced by social manipulation. Thus we can envisage wholesale programmes of social engineering, formulated to achieve planned results, without consideration for the beliefs or consciences of the individual members of society.

The only protection against such a view is an untiring emphasis on the unique dignity of every human individual, however odd or mistaken they seem to us. And it is to stress the independence of moral claims from any social structure or psychological mechanism; to root them in a reality set in critical opposition to any and every society – in the reality of a transcendent God, for theists; and in the reality of the *dharma*, the true way to freedom from passion and sorrow, for Buddhists. In order to free our moral beliefs from any form of authoritarianism or irrationalism, we do not need theories that deny the unique value of human life and the absolute importance of truth, reason and understanding. In that way, we only substitute one form of irrationalism for another. We liberate mankind from a tyrant God, in order to deliver him into the hands of passion and the will to power. What we need is a firmer grasp of what religious revelation really is, a keener understanding of the God who requires of us nothing but love, or of the possibility of an enlightenment which releases us from passion. God is no tyrant or infantile authority, nor is He one who will take from us what He has given, our irreplaceable and unique individuality, our responsibility for determining our own futures, and our hope for the realization of a goal of supreme knowledge and bliss.

I would want to assert very firmly that we have much to learn about human nature from Nietzsche, from Darwin, from Freud and from Marx. We would be foolish indeed if we brushed them aside, or failed to recognize the great insights they have brought. Nevertheless, the general philosophy of scientific objectivism that has been forged out of their thoughts has to be recognized as an attack upon some of our deepest beliefs about human existence and destiny. It is an attack upon God and upon any idea of purpose in creation. It is an attack upon absolute moral values, and upon any idea that duty can be a supremely overriding reason for action. It is an attack upon the soul, and upon the idea that every human individual is of unique and irreplaceable worth. I have argued that scientific objectivism is not, in fact, soundly based upon scientific evidence, but that it relies upon vastly over-generalized theories that mistake the nature and limits of the heuristic explanatory models used in the natural sciences. And I have argued that the moral consequences of the theories are such that even their propounders cannot seriously accept them. Indeed, they are rejected in the very formulations of the theories themselves. It is the absolute reverence for truth and reason that has led to the view that truth and reason themselves are projections of human interest and not moral absolutes. Something has plainly gone wrong. And a closer consideration of just what has gone wrong may well cause us to think very seriously again about the existence of the soul, about moral absolutes and about God. Maybe the truth is that the scientific, objective attitude cannot be applied consistently to human beings, who always remain transcendent subjects of knowledge and responsible action. But that attitude is morally required of human subjects, as they seek to understand their world and extend their capacities for responsible action within it. Scientific objectivism only goes wrong, in other words, when it claims to give a *complete* account of the world and of human existence. Talk of 'the soul' helps us to remember that, especially in our intelligent understanding and our moral striving, we always transcend the objects we can rationally understand and responsibly deal with. Of course, the human soul is not some sort of disembodied spirit, floating just above our heads. It is firmly embodied in very particular and definite biological, psychological and social contexts. Yet it remains a spiritual – that is, not observable or scientifically definable – subject in that complex, ordered world. The mistake of scientific objectivism is to reduce it wholly to an element of the objective world. And it is noteworthy that each science tends to claim omnicompetence for itself, by making the soul an element of its own particular scheme, whether biological, psychological or sociological. We need to resist all such attempts to encompass the soul, and thereby remember that there are depths to existence that the sciences can never plumb.

The basic distinguishing capacity of the soul is its capacity to grasp and understand truth and to act responsibly in the light of such understanding. But the unique dignity of the soul lies in its freedom to determine itself by such understanding or not. It is in such self-determination that a person really expresses what he takes himself to be – not just theoretically, but in a practical awareness of himself. In sincere moral commitment, a person affirms his transcendence of all material conditions.

To choose to do something simply because it is right is to give a distinctive and particular worth to human life, a worth quite unique and distinct from that of happiness or desire. Human beings can and must make a fundamental choice between good and evil (which is, in fact, a lesser or more partial good). Such a choice is an ultimate commitment of the will, and it is finally beyond any determination by material factors of either character or circumstance.

I believe that everyone does know that justice and goodness must be pursued for their own sakes, as surely as they know that physical objects or other minds exist. Yet the nature of that 'must' is so unique and peculiar that it eludes all attempts to explain it in any other terms whatsoever. The good ought to be done. But why? What is the nature of that peculiar constraint, by which the soul feels itself to be bound – even though it is always able to ignore or turn from it in action?

I believe that the only tenable view of the matter is that here the human soul finds itself confronted by an overriding claim. It is not a mere command; it is not a matter of free decision; it is quite unique in kind; something that calls us to deny the claims of self-interest and act for the sake of good alone. But does such a view really make sense? Not, I think, for a thoroughgoing materialist. There is no place in his world of unconscious, purposeless collisions of energy for such extremely peculiar 'objective moral claims'.

But the theist has to be careful, too. We should not say that these claims are just the commands of God, as though they were morally neutral orders and we can then decide whether or not to carry them out. What we must say is that, in our experience, we find ourselves confronted by values we know to be worthy of choice for their own sakes, but the choice of which requires of us a conquest of desire and inclination. The moral life consists in the subordination of desire to value.

And yet, of course, that value is always value for someone, or for some group of people. Justice, fidelity and love are realized between people, in the form of their relationships. It is those forms of relationship that we choose, in choosing value. We should choose them for their own sakes, whatever our own inclinations happen to be. The basic question is: is there a place for such objective claims in our view of the world? Is it really intelligible for us to commend the choice of value, even in opposition to inclination? To speak of the subordination of self-interest to duty and value?

I believe that to make sense of this sort of belief, we have to see the soul as finding its proper and distinctive mode of being in self-transcendence – in overcoming the temptations of self-interest, and learning to be conformed to the love of virtue. In other words, we have to see in moral commitment the proper fulfilment of human life. And such a view only fully makes sense when we can see value, not just as some abstract, hypothetical or merely possible state in the future, but as a living, present, transforming reality now. It only makes sense when we see an actual value and perfection that attracts us by its inherent beauty, which draws us towards itself by the power of love.

For then we are not simply aiming at some abstraction, but we are seeking to relate to a goal of supreme value, which theists call 'God', and which Buddhists call *nirvana*. St Augustine put the point exactly when he said, 'I hold virtue to be nothing else than perfect love of God'.[1] When God or some real and supreme goal of action is rejected, it is very difficult to make sense of the life of virtue. Of course, we know that we should do what is right for its own sake. Yet there is something odd about divorcing duty entirely from inclination, or setting it in opposition to inclination, to what will bring human life to its highest fulfilment.

The British philosopher Peter Geach even says that the sense of duty is a dangerous and irrational thing. He quotes an earlier philosopher, Bradley, with approval: 'This sense of duty is empty self-will and self-assurance.'[2] And he adds, 'There is no good sense to be made of an appeal . . . to the Sense of Duty . . . a rational consideration propounded to an agent must . . . relate to his Inclinations'.[3] We might very well feel – a great many moral philosophers have felt – that it does not make sense to do anything unless it will in some way pay us, in the end. Certainly, if ethics is something we invent, or a set of rules we just make up, it is hard to see why we should make up rules that might very well go against our inclinations. Would we not rather make up rules that will give us as much of what we want as can be reasonably managed?

If God is rejected, it is tempting for philosophers to found rational morality upon some form of 'social contract' – a set of social rules everyone could agree to live by. It is, after all, in everyone's interests to have general moral laws, in order to get a secure and stable society in which they can pursue their own ends. That is true, but there is no reason why such laws should be invested with the awe and reverence accorded to the traditional 'moral law'. They are simply rules made up by some members of a society to ensure social order. They must be obeyed because, if they are not, the culprit will be punished, if he is caught. What exactly the rules are, and how they are enforced, does not matter very much as long as a reasonable degree of order results from their existence. As the great English legal theorist Austin put it, 'laws are commands of a sovereign, backed by sanctions'.[4] The sovereign commands what laws he will; the only question is whether the available sanctions are effective in preserving order in society, and letting us go about our own business.

In this situation, the rational course is to support the law, while seeking to take advantage of its loopholes, or break it when you can get away with it. Most people will be best off if everyone else obeys the law while they do not. So all rational people will seek to break the law if they can. But they will also seek to make it as hard for everyone to break the law as is necessary to preserve social order. This is a realistic view, but it is hardly calculated to lead to a very great respect for morality. Indeed, the appeal to social justice may rightly be seen as a sort of confidence trick – a means of getting others to respect values one would personally, in secret, try to evade.

The influential philosopher Philippa Foot says, 'Nothing can rationally persuade us to a course of action unless it can be shown to fulfil our desires or interests'.[5] On such a view, we will still have moral rules and standards. We will have general laws for keeping peace and order in society. And we will have those professional standards of conduct that make social institutions possible – honesty between businessmen and confidentiality in medicine, and so on. Nevertheless, the role of morality will be a very limited one. It will pay most of us to keep the rules and conform to the standards of our profession, since we will suffer if we do not. But there is nothing much wrong with a little bending of the rules. And, if we are strong and resourceful enough, it will be quite rational to use or break them for our own ends. The successful criminal will be supremely rational in pursuing his own interests, and he will probably be a pillar of society, too. At least for the strong, the calculated pursuit of hypocrisy is the logical conclusion of social-contract theory, wherever it really is, as it often claims, based on rational self-interest.

Some moral philosophers hold that reason does not lead to self-interest at all, however. They try to find a basis for morality founded on reason alone, not on any religious or metaphysical beliefs. Professor R. M. Hare,[6] of Oxford University, and Professor John Rawls, of Harvard,[7] are key spokesmen for this view. Reason, they say, is based on impartiality, and on the principle that whatever goes for one person must apply to anybody in a similar situation. So a truly rational principle will not just consider my own interests. It will consider everyone's interests equally and impartially, and see that whatever I prescribe for myself must be prescribed to anybody else in a similar case. So reason leads us to put ourselves in others' shoes, consider their inclinations, and work out a general system for maximizing everyone's interests, in general. If we are purely rational, we will see that the pleasure of each person is as important as the pleasure of every other person. So what reason decrees is the equitable pursuit of pleasure by all, not the selfish pursuit of pleasure by me.

This theory can sound persuasive, but there is obviously something wrong with it. No doubt a computer, without desires or personal feelings of pleasure, could set up a system of rules that were totally impartial. But people are not computers; they are animals with strong desires; and what is really rational for them is to satisfy those desires as effectively as possible.

Somebody may indeed desire to aim at the pleasure of others – altruism is not impossible. But if it does not happen to be one of your desires, there is nothing in the bare appeal to reason that can persuade you to have it. In fact, when you think of it, the idea that the happiness of some totally unknown person in a faraway country is to be considered just as important as your own happiness is ludicrous; the idea that you should consider other people's children to be as important as your own is quite unacceptable.

In practice, of course, theories like these get very sophisticated – they have to, to make any sense at all. But their basic flaw is quite simple. It lies in the claim that what reason decrees is action on purely impartial and universal principles. In one sense of 'reason' that is true – the sense in which we can imagine a purely impartial, uninvolved calculating machine, setting out to order human life in accordance with the most efficient and economical set of general rules. But the question is: why should human beings live by such a purely abstract calculus? Most of them are not going to, in any case, so the actual world in which we live will be one of competing self-interest and strong emotions. In a world of violent and compulsive emotion, the pure rationalist appears impractical and Utopian. His abstract principles do not move anyone and fasten on to no emotion. The idea that we should always act impartially is a recipe for defeat, in the ruthless competition of human action. In a war, we cannot be impartial; we have to be committed. And human life is a war, however disguised and demilitarized – a war between the passions and interests of different individuals and groups, all of them partial and to some degree irrational.

This sort of liberal rationalism is in fact a decayed form of theism, which sees the uniqueness of humanity in its possession of reason. In so far as reason is seen as the proper distinguishing mark of humans, an appeal to universal principles will succeed in having some effect. But if it is believed that the universe is not founded on reason; that humans are the products simply of chance mutation; and that there is no special significance in being moral – then the appeal to universal principles will fall on deaf ears. 'Yes', it will be said, 'that is how a purely rational being would act. But whatever else we are, we are not purely rational. Our principles must be modified in the light of our passions.' Why should the person of heroic will be bound by the universal rules he endorses for all those weaker than himself? The morality of universal prin-ciples is for machines or angels and not for men.

So the attempt to establish a purely rational morality, not founded on any supernatural sanctions or metaphysical beliefs, is doomed to fail. And that is basically because reason itself seems to show its marginal character in human life. 'Once one has become adjusted to the idea that we are here because we have evolved from simple chemical compounds by a process of natural selection,' says Francis Crick, one of the discoverers of the structure of DNA, 'it is remarkable how many of the problems of the modern world take on a completely new light.'[8] Reason, he thinks, can show the basis of morality in a set of survival-oriented drive-inhibitory mechanisms. They give rise to the bonds of love and loyalty, arising out of re-directed aggression and fear instincts. Knowing this, reason can help us to be free from the sense of compulsion and abso-luteness of the 'moral' impulses. It is hardly likely to produce a new compulsion, to act on purely rational principles, even when they go against our needs and desires. It is much more likely to lead us towards a working adjustment between the various compulsions and desires we are landed with. No sort of morality can any longer be viewed as absolutely imperative – not the traditional imperatives and not the principles of abstract reason either. The sense of binding moral obligation, and of the uniqueness of the human soul in responding to it, will disappear in the rising tide of realization that human beings are without purpose, without uniqueness, without future, in a world originating by chance and ruled by necessity.

It seems, then, that the attempt to found morality on a social contract, on long-term inclination or on impartial reason alone, is unlikely to succeed. We cannot avoid the question of how some sense of compelling moral obligation can fit into our view of the world. The difficulty, as we have seen, is that duty cannot be divorced from inclination, and yet inclination cannot be a sufficient foundation for duty. In the end, only the existence of a reality of supreme value, which is the goal of human morality, can resolve this difficulty in a coherent way. Theists call this reality 'God', and once one sees that, one sees that God cannot command things arbitrarily or irrationally. His commands are indeed absolute, but they are meant for our good. It is in obeying them that we find our proper, our highest good, that we fulfil the purpose of our creation. Moreover, our obedience and our realization of the good are not just externally related — as if God gave us a reward for doing what He said. In moral obedience, we are not just obeying some impersonal law or principle. If we could see fully and truly, we would see that, in moral obedience, we are putting ourselves in relation to a personal God of supreme value and perfection. In His commands, God shows us something of His own being; what we discern is something of His absolute perfection, judging our own imperfection and drawing us on towards itself.

So, when we discern something of the reality of God, in and through the moral ambiguities of the world, we are naturally drawn towards the perfection we see, and we realize that, in being conformed to it, we will realize what we were created to be. It is our vision and understanding that shapes our inclinations, and not the other way round. It is in the context of such a vision that the moral life fully makes sense. When we lose sight of God, the various parts of the moral life disintegrate. Though they may remain, they no longer form a coherent pattern. They are strange, inexplicable feelings or compulsions we can neither rid ourselves of nor properly explain. Thus we know that we must commit ourselves to justice and truth for their own sakes, and not just for what they may bring us. But we cannot render this knowledge fully intelligible to ourselves. It does not fit into the world-view of scientific objectivism, even though that world-view is founded upon it, albeit one-sidedly.

The sense of absolute moral obligation is a reminiscence of God; the sense of duty is the remembrance of destroyed love. To recover it in its full context and meaning, we have to see that the soul is called to be conformed to understanding and love of reality (and thereby to justice and truth), and that is because reality, for the theist, unfolds itself as capable of being understood and loved, as intelligible and beautiful, as the expression of a supremely perfect and personal God. We have to see that the soul finds its proper being and fulfilment in obedience to such a call; that it is not an alien intrusion into a world of blind uncaring energy, but a subject of rational consciousness, responding to a supreme Subjectivity that underlies and is expressed in all material things. The sense of absolute claim; the sense of response and encounter; the sense of possible fulfilment through such response – these are all integral parts of the experience of the soul, by which it knows its own transcendence of all material forms, and its innermost reality as a continual response to a supreme and self-existent value.

If we see these things clearly, the reign of scientific objectivism, which is a hangover from nineteenth-century secularism, will be over. Yet there are still certain trends in modern thought, particularly in neurophysiology and in cybernetics, which may seem to threaten the reinstatement of any idea of the spirituality of the soul. In the next chapter, I will examine these trends, which are sometimes taken to prove the complete dependence of the soul upon material mechanisms of the brain. I hope to show that any such alleged proofs have as little chance of success as the other forms of biological, psychological and sociological reductionism that have been considered so far.

7

THE SOUL
AND THE BRAIN

ONE OF THE MOST PERSUASIVE attacks on the idea of the soul comes from those who would claim that the soul depends wholly for its existence on the brain, which can be understood in straightforward physical terms. The brain, it might be said, is just like a rather complex computer, and it can be predicted, modified or controlled in the same sort of way. We do not talk about computers having souls; so we need not talk about human beings having souls, either. Souls are superfluous; we should just see the brain as a complicated electrochemical computer, and treat it accordingly. There is no 'ghost in the machine', it might be said; no need to talk about hidden or secret spiritual entities. There is just the machine, and we will soon be able to understand and control that with the aid of science.

Neurophysiology, the analysis of the physical structure of the brain, is still an infant science. But it has already reached a stage at which certain sorts of experiences can be chemically induced, or certain personality traits surgically altered. The rather drastic operation of prefrontal leucotomy, for example, which separates the frontal lobes from the rest of the brain, has consequences that include major personality changes. It seems that we can change character by tampering with the brain.

Monkeys have been sexually stimulated by passing electric currents to exposed parts of the cortex. By the same methods, bulls can be halted in the middle of an aggressive charge, hens can be made to fly in panic or display sexually. Further, human subjects with electrodes implanted in their brains can be caused to see such things as red patches when they are electrically stimulated, and by stimulating different parts of the cortex, different sorts of sensations can be caused.

From such facts as these, it may seem that conscious experiences are all caused by electrical stimulation of parts of the brain, and that they could in principle be artificially produced by such stimulation. As well as electrical stimulation, many chemicals are regularly used by psychiatrists in the course of their daily work, in order to relieve depressive illnesses or acute anxiety states. The use of stimulants and depressants is almost normal in our society. And it is probable that more extensive control of moods, of bad temper and aggression, of happiness or misery, could be induced by more efficient methods of drug control. We may have here a much more effective method of controlling human behaviour than our present course of moral persuasion and exhortation. Where, in the past, people may have looked for some spiritual answer to depression, they may find more certain and rapid relief by a simple injection or course of tablets.

The fact that drugs, surgery and electrical stimulation can alter your experiences and character, and that the physical structure of the brain will perhaps be completely understood some day, has great implications for our view of human life. Just as we can now transplant hearts, kidneys or other physical organs, we may learn to transplant brains, and thus transfer a person from one body to another. Not only that, but we might learn to duplicate, artificially, the structure of a person's brain – perhaps making an exact replica of it in metal or silicone – and so give that 'person' immortality. And if we could do that, we could manufacture any number of duplicates of the same person. Then we might be able to control their behaviour from some central computer, so that they would do whatever we want without complaint – since we would control all their thoughts and desires by controlling their brain impulses.

All this is in the realm of science fiction, of course. But some scientists think it is possible. And, if it is possible, it seems to show that all our experience is totally dependent on physical states of our brains. That humane thinker Julian Huxley writes, 'I confidently look forward to a time when eugenic improvement will become one of the major aims of mankind'.[1] He is thinking of developing control of the genetic basis of human life, by manipulating the DNA that forms the basis of character, so that we might be able to eliminate aggression, increase intelligence and altruism and so on. But it is clear that such control will be even more effective if we can learn to control the brain directly, and thus cause people to be altruistic, aggressive, happy or depressed as we choose, by pressing an array of buttons. In the end, we could insert experiences, emotions and even seeming memories into their minds. The degree of control that will be possible seems frightening. It looks as if the species *homo sapiens* will be able to design and manufacture its own descendants to a planned recipe. Complete conscious control over character and experience may at last become a fact.

What happens, in view of these quite astonishing possibilities, to the idea of the human soul? When we see the possibility of controlling human nature by physical means; of duplicating persons or mixing their memories up, even transferring memories from one person to another; of changing characters, desires and hopes at will – what then happens to the idea of a spiritual, indivisible soul? The more we realize the extent of the dependence of personal consciousness upon physical brain-states, the less plausible seems the idea that we each have one unique and continuing subject of moral will and awareness, which is our soul. So we need to look rather carefully at these claims and possibilities.

In the first place, it is not really surprising that if we interfere with the brain by cutting pieces out of it, putting electric shocks through it or injecting strange chemical substances into it, our personality and experience will be affected. Nobody would be surprised if we reminded them that, if we chopped their heads off, their conscious experience would be badly affected. Similarly, if I lock someone in a dark room for three years, I would expect his character to change for the worse. Do drastic things to people, and they will be affected quite badly. So it is not odd to be told that our experiences and characters depend greatly on our environment, on the states of our bodies and brains. If our bodies lack one chemical, we get diabetes and feel tired and lethargic. If they lack another, we may feel very depressed; and both states can be relieved by taking the necessary chemical artificially.

This is not worrying; it is obvious, when you think about it. The worry only comes in when the claim is made that *all* a person's experiences are determined *solely* by physical states of the brain, and that these states follow inevitable, predictable laws of physics and chemistry alone. B. A. Farrell, who was a psychologist at Oxford University, once said, 'A human being is a modulator of pulse frequencies, and nothing more'.[2] We have met that 'nothing more' before. This time, man is being seen as a very complex feedback, storage and reaction machine, and nothing more; a computer of a relatively advanced sort, with an organic main-frame.

If this were true, it would, I think, be worrying. If I am able to predict with certainty, by using known physical laws, all subsequent movement of a person's brain, then I would know exactly what he was going to do, and I would know that he could not do otherwise. People may think they are acting 'freely', that they have choices. But in fact all their thoughts and acts would follow inevitably from physical laws alone. Once we know that, we should really give up all notions of responsibility and guilt, of punishment and desert, and simply set out to control deviant behaviour in the most effective way. Law courts would be replaced by panels of psychiatrists and brain surgeons, and the only question to ask would be how to modify the person's behaviour so that he did more acceptable things in future. I think I would find this more worrying than being brought before a jury; the possibilities for social manipulation are enormous.

But the basic question is, are all my experiences caused by brain-states that are wholly predictable according to laws of physics? If we believe that persons are free to direct their own lives, at least to some extent, we will normally think that their actions are not wholly predictable or explicable in physical terms. The quite widely held view that freedom and complete physical predictability are wholly compatible seems to me another version of the double-think view that we can go on assuming that people often could have done otherwise (as we do in English law, for example) even when we know that they could not have done so in fact.

If I am right, there seems to be a test for whether people are free. For if we did manage to predict all a person's acts in physical terms alone, we would have shown that real moral freedom – the physically indeterminate choice of action – did not exist, at least in that case. But in fact we can say with certainty that such a test could never be carried out. The amount of information we would need, to be able to predict all a person's subsequent behaviour, is infinite. It cannot even be quantified exactly enough to form the basis of accurate prediction. We cannot keep people in closely controlled laboratory conditions for long. And we can never be sure we have exhaustively specified all possible causal influences on their behaviour. In view of these severe limitations on our ability to gather adequate data, we will have to retreat to rather vague generalizations about probabilities. We may be able to predict roughly how large masses of people will react to various stimuli (though economists and politicians do not seem to be very good at it). But we will never be able to predict exactly how individuals will behave. We can say what our friends are *likely* to do, but we can never be absolutely sure. So, though at first sight there seems to be a scientific test for whether freedom exists, it turns out that no such test could ever be successfully devised or carried out.

So I could never *prove* that all my brain-states are predictable solely by appeal to the laws of physics. But may they nevertheless *be* so? Perhaps we can begin to consider this by looking at the well-known analogy of a computer. Computers do, of course, obey the laws of physics. If they did not, we could never be sure that they would work. Once the program is loaded, we can predict what the computer will do. But we will nevertheless not understand what it is really doing, if we only know the laws of physics and nothing more. All we will have is a series of physical states, following general sequences. What we can never know, from the laws of physics alone, is what the whole series is *for*; what it *means*; or *why* it was set up in the first place.

Moreover, the initial state of the series of physical events has been determined by a designed program, which is not part of the system, and which, again, can only be understood in terms of human purposes and desires. And, of course, most programs require continuous humanly regulated input, which can then be processed by the hard-wired systems in the computer. So it is not true that all events in the computer can be predicted according to laws of physics alone. The initial design of the system; the more-or-less continuous interface with human input; and the interpretation of the data produced by the system are all non-derivable from a study of the closed physical structure of the computer itself.

The model of complete physical predictability is, it must be stressed, an ideal, hypothetical abstraction from a complex, dynamic, emergent reality. We should not think of mental activity as an 'interference' in a closed mechanistic causal web. It is the idea of such a web that is a pure imaginative construction of the mind. What is being said is this: imagine that the world consists only of so many physical particles, with clearly definable properties, relating to each other according to a few general laws. Nothing else ever interferes with this system – it is closed, in that sense. Since we can know all the laws and properties exhaustively, and there can never be any new ones or any new, unique, truly creative events, everything in that system is perfectly predictable.

In laboratories or very simple environments, like the near vacuum of space, we can come close to having such a closed system. In such places, our ideal model is close to reality. But in environments where things get much more complicated – like the surface of the earth – the model begins to break down. We have to ask: do we really know all the properties of physical particles, exhaustively? We might think of a physical property as a tendency or capacity to react to other forces in specific ways. Thus what we call 'mass' is the capacity to interact with other objects by repelling or attracting them in special ways. Particles may have many properties – sub-atomic physicists seem to discover more patterns of interaction every day. We may think of them as forces locked up in the structure of the particle, ready to be realized if an appropriate interaction occurs. So the properties we perceive a particle to have depend on the sorts of interactions it has with other particles. How can we ever be sure we have catalogued these exhaustively? Quite simply, we cannot. So the first point to make is that we can never know if we have found all the properties even of quite simple physical objects.

But then it gets worse, for physical objects become very complex. They form complex structures, hierarchies of organization and pattern. May such complexity not call into play new properties, new forms of interaction, which had not previously existed? This possibility certainly cannot be excluded in principle. It is just a dogma that the laws of physics are set immutably the same for ever. I do not mind accepting the dogma that the basic laws of physics will not change drastically. But I do not see why we should believe that there cannot also be other, more complex laws of relationship at higher levels of physical complexity – especially since that is what things actually look like. There is an alternative model for the physical world: that is the model of organic development. On the basis of rather simple and general laws, more complex structures come into existence, with correspondingly more complex patterns of interaction between them. These structures not only exhibit law-like behaviour (which implies regularity and repetitiveness), they also exhibit something analogous to creative response to stimuli (which allows for uniqueness and originality).

For this model, the human brain would be a particularly complex structure, with a dominant organizing position in the body, whose interactions generate new, emergent properties (of consciousness) and correspondingly new and unpredictable forms of response (in terms of desire and purpose). The important point is that conscious states are not just thrown up as a sort of irrelevant by-product of brain-activity, which itself carries on in the same old mechanistic, predictable way. Rather, conscious states will be emergent properties of the physical system, and as such, they will modify radically the nature of the system. They will enter into the pattern of interactions that make up physical reality. Its laws will still, if you like, be physical, but they will not be derivable from the simple general principles of inorganic physics. To understand them, the concepts of intention, interpretation and rational deliberation have to be introduced; otherwise, you simply cannot see what is truly going on.

Consider a person going through a simple deductive argument, like a piece of arithmetic. Obviously, this causes his brain to operate. It seems equally obvious that the brain processes will be guided by states and patterns of interaction that physics does not deal with – states of understanding the concepts of number, patterns of change directed by principles of logical connection, rather than simple causal regularity. Is it not simpler to say that these states and patterns of change are states of the *same* reality that also has physically locatable cells and forces like electromagnetic charge and mass? The fact is simply that when those forces assume the complex form of organization of the human brain, new emergent states and principles are generated, and these continually modify the total state of the brain, making its states unpredictable from laws of physics alone.

Some people might call this a form of materialism, because we are saying that consciousness and brain are different ways of looking at the same total reality. But, of course, if we are really saying that consciousness and the brain are the same, then we could put this by saying that the brain is the outward expression of consciousness. That is, mind and brain are not two quite different, disconnected realities. They form parts of one integrated whole, in which the brain is the way the soul appears to others. As far as we can see the situation the soul is generated by a particular physical system. At a specific point in time, a subject of rational consciousness comes into being. All conscious states belong to a subject, which is able to understand, deliberate, formulate goals and initiate actions. Its perceptions are perceptions of the physical world; its intentions are enacted within it. As Aquinas said, 'The soul in a certain fashion demands the body in order to act'[3] and in order to get information. Should we say, then, that the soul *is* the brain? That would probably be too crude a view, for it might mislead us into thinking that all conscious states were determined by predictable laws of physics alone, or by brain-states as thus predictable. All our evidence shows that this is not the case; for our conscious processes often seem to be causally primary. Moreover, the subject of consciousness is capable in principle of substantial existence; and therefore of continued existence in some other form of body.

The most important characteristic of the soul is its capacity for transcendence. It has the capacity to 'exist', to stand outside the physical processes that generate it, and of which it is part. We might see the soul, the subject of awareness, deliberation and intention, as one part of a vast web of interacting processes, at various degrees of complexity, coming to conscious perception of the actions of other forces upon it; and realizing its own capacities in accordance with more or less clearly formulated principles. It is distinguished, not by being quite different in kind from its material environment, but by reflecting and acting in that environment in a more conscious, goal-oriented way. In other words, the soul is not an alien intrusion into a mechanistic world. It is the culmination and realization of the principles that dimly inform what we call 'matter' at every stage of its existence. Yet, in that culmination, it is able also to transcend the material. The material is limited to a particular location in space and time. It is contained by that location. But the soul by nature 'transcends'; it is orientated away from itself, to what is beyond itself.

When we apprehend a truth we do not simply register sensations, passively. We rather seek by intelligent enquiry to understand something of the nature of things, of how things really are in their characters and relationships. To grasp a truth is to grasp something that transcends particularity and self-concern. It is to grasp what is impartial, objective, universal. Of course truths are uttered in particular languages, from limited viewpoints, but they aim at the universal and comprehensive. Truth always lies beyond us, in its fullness. Yet we discern something of it, as soon as we move beyond the passive and particular, towards an active grasp of properties and relations. In understanding '$E = Mc^2$', we move in a realm with its own norms and constraints, transcending what appears, to grasp or move towards what may be and the inner form and structure of what is.

This apprehension of truth, which is most characteristic of the soul, is far from being aesthetically or morally neutral. In physics, we seek the elegant, the beautiful, the simple and the fruitful theory. The intellectual structures we seek are structures of beauty. And they impose their moral constraints – of impartiality, comprehensiveness, honesty and trust in one another. Without these values, science as a progressive body of knowledge could not exist. They are internal to the activity of truth-seeking, and that activity is a search for a beauty of order, form and structure which we seek to discover, apprehend and contemplate.

The world of 'bare sense-experience', so beloved of the older sort of empiricists, is a world without beauty or value or truth – all these things became conventions or emotional projections. But we may discern a realm in which truth has attracting beauty and compelling value, both repressing self-interest and calling forth a flowering of understanding, an ecstasis of the soul, finding its true fulfilment in the discernment of value.

All this may seem rather intellectualist. But the doctrine of the soul reminds us that it is not only in the supreme creativity of Einstein or Beethoven that we touch the realm of spirit through the veils of sense. They are supreme adventurers of the spirit, but each of us can distinguish, in our own way, between truth and falsehood; beauty and squalor; the worthwhile and the trivial; love and selfishness. We may not be able to do differential calculus, but we can distort the truth by resentment or prejudice, or we can try to be fair and honest. We can litter the country or cherish it. We can get permanently drunk or take a pride in painting the house. We can go all out to make money or look after the old lady next door. It is in such simple ways that we shape our souls, and it is in these ways that our intelligence is exercised morally, that we can all assert our transcendence over impulse and natural inclination. The transcendence of the soul is its self-determination towards the true, the beautiful and the good. Ultimately, it is its determination towards that which is most fully perfect and actual, the supremely real and good.

For all this to be true, it is not necessary that there should be a strange ghost hidden in the machine of the body. The fact is that the brain is not a machine, as most contemporary computers undoubtedly are. However sophisticated our 'expert systems' are, in computer science, these are still basically machines that operate mechanically in accordance with complex purposes, rational programs and final interpretations of results, all of which are external to the computer mechanism, in human operators. In the brain, however, the purpose, deliberation and interpretation are internal to the system; and that means that this 'physical system' includes states and operates in accordance with principles not covered by laws of physics alone. Indeed, in its subjectivity and transcendence, each soul is beyond the reach of any general inductive laws – for each

one contains new and unique properties whose effects on sur-
rounding phenomena cannot be exactly predicted from past
experience.

What we have to grasp is the vast complexity of reality –
the way it surpasses any set of precise laws or descriptions we
apply to it; the organic interrelatedness of events – so that
every event is affected by and in turn affects every other event
in some, maybe infinitesimal, degree; and the creatively
emergent character of physical processes – the way their interactions create new, emergent properties, which modify the
process of change in future. This general view of nature, which
seems to be fully corroborated by such developments in
physics as quantum theory and relativity theory, helps us to see
mental states and operations as emerging from the physical
structure of the brain, and modifying it in new ways. The soul
is the subject of these states and operations; and, like a
butterfly emerging from a chrysalis, it may be able to disentangle itself from the public spatial properties of the brain and
exist either alone or in a different form of materialization.

Immortality is, on this view, a real possibility. It follows
from what I have been saying that we could, in theory, make
artificial intelligence machines, super-computers, which really
would have souls. That is, they would have states of conscious
understanding, freedom and moral responsibility, and relationship to God (as I have put it, 'determination towards supreme
value'). In fact, I do not see why we should deny that possibility. We bring souls into existence whenever we have children.
We can now fertilize embryos in laboratories, so that our
control over procreation is increasing. It is possible, in theory,
to construct a genetic sequence, which will begin embryonic
development and so create a human life artificially. It is not
out of the question that we could also construct a replica of
such sequences in other forms, and so create quite new sorts of
souls.

Of course, if we did so, we would have just the same sorts
of responsibility to those souls as we now have to human
beings. We would have to respect and care for them, treat

them as responsible and ascribe personal rights to them. It would be grossly immoral to treat them simply as machines, even if they looked like machines. They would indeed be persons. So there is nothing much to worry about in the rather science-fiction idea of creating metal computer-persons. If such things were wholly controllable and predictable, because of some program we had put into them, then we know they are not persons at all, however cunningly they may be made to deceive. But if they really are free, rational and responsible, then we cannot wholly control them without infringing their truly personal rights and destroying that freedom.

Of course, there are very good reasons why such beings may never be produced. The sorts of experimentation that would be necessary to make them would be morally abhorrent. And the sort of dictatorship that would be needed to exercise such total control over personal beings is itself so undesirable that it should always be resisted. So we are not likely to get computer-persons in the foreseeable future. But there seems nothing absurd in the idea that souls, persons, could be brought into being by the construction and development of suitable material states. After all, that is just what happens in the growth of every human embryo. Subjects of rational consciousness are generated by material systems, by natural processes of emergent causation; and there is no need for believers to deny it.

What is wrong with materialism is that it takes much too low a view of matter. It sees it just in terms of its simplest, most abstract and repetitive, measurable and publicly observable properties. This analytical approach has, it is true, been of immense value in producing an exact quantitative set of models for explaining and predicting natural processes. But it is very strange that the limits of the approach, which are quite obvious to anyone who tries to apply quantitative predictive models to human affairs (to any economist, for example), have sometimes been ignored. For the truth is that 'matter' has much greater potential, complexity, opacity to quantitative measurement,

uniqueness and novelty than can be expressed in any set of scientific models, whether considered singly or together. Indeed,
we might say that 'matter' will only be fully understood when it
is seen in its innermost tendency towards consciousness and
realization of value. It will only be understood truly in terms of
its end or goal; its fullest realization, and not its simplest initial
states.

In this process, human beings stand at the transition-point
at which matter turns outwards from itself towards a transcendent source of truth, beauty and goodness. The Bible puts it
supremely well when it says, 'The Lord God took some soil
from the ground and formed a man out of it; he breathed life-
giving breath into his nostrils and the man began to live'.[4]
Man is made of dust; but he is filled with the spirit of God. He
emerges from the simplest material forms, but finds his true
kinship in the goal and fulfilment of his existence, the supreme
Goodness.

The trouble many people have about the soul lies in a particular picture they have of it. They think of God making a
complete spiritual thing, with its own personality, and then
having to attach it to some physical body. The soul has a
purely external relation to the body. Whereas the biblical
account is that man is a truly physical entity, touched with
God's spirit. It is *this holistic entity* that knows and thinks and
decides; yet this entity is more than electrons or chemicals or
genes or psychological states or social roles. All those
elements enter into what it is, but none of them, singly or
together, exhaust what it is. That is why it is, after all, misleading to say that it is this *body* that thinks – because when we
think of a body we think of a corpse, not a living thinking
thing. So when we speak of the soul, we speak of this physical
entity in its capacity for responsible relation to God, or to
those values of truth and beauty through which God is present,
often unrecognized.

But if this is true, how can the soul exist without a body?
The material universe has produced out of itself states of consciousness and processes of reasoning and intentional action.

Now many physical properties that are parts of a more complex whole can exist separately, or in another whole that is significantly different. There is no trouble about that – the molecules making up my foot could exist in a chair or tree. So why could conscious states not exist apart from the brain? The difficulty lies in the fact that conscious states are not just strung together, like beads on a thread, each one separate and externally connected to the others. Each experience needs to be placed in the context of many others, recognized and interpreted. It is the experience of some subject, which relates all the various experiences it has, and organizes them within a set of projects and aims. Experiences form a unity, in being the experiences of one common subject. They cannot simply be taken out of that unity, and inserted somewhere else, for then their character would be different. It is, therefore, not the conscious states that can exist separately, but the subject that knows and remembers these states and has certain dispositions and goals. This subject is acquainted with physical realities, and its goals are formed by and rooted in physical realities. It has its place in the physical world; it has a locatable viewpoint and field of action, in space. Yet it is itself beyond every spatial and publicly observable description; it is the subject that is never an object, even to itself; the agent that is never itself an event in the world.

It is essential to see that the soul is both a spiritual and an embodied reality. It is not a ghost behind the scenes, and it is not just the physical brain, in its publicly describable properties. It is not an object or event or set of events in the world. It is a point of subjectivity and transcendence, of rational understanding and responsible action, which comes to be at a particular stage of the emergent interactions of spatial, material substances. Once it is generated, it continues to have a place in those physical interactions, to respond to them and realize itself in them, as their 'actuating principle', as Aquinas put it. It would seem that, though it has a real and distinctive form of existence, it must have something to actuate; the 'form' must be the form of something other than itself.

Nevertheless, in its understanding the soul relates itself also to that realm of truth and value that transcends the physical; in its interior life of feeling, and perhaps of prayer and contemplation, it expresses a capacity and natural tendency to relate to a purely spiritual realm. Each subject is one, throughout its known and remembered states, in the continuous development of its projects and its acceptance of responsibility for past acts. The 'bare subject' is an abstraction, which never exists alone. But it is an essential element of the whole, binding together the organic unity within a whole of developing apprehensions and responses. And this subject is not confined by its physical boundaries. In understanding and imagination, it ranges beyond the temporal and actual, considering possibilities and values, capable of discerning the eternal and infinite hidden in the forms of time and place.

Thus, though it is truly material, there is a very real sense in which the soul looks beyond the material world for its proper fulfilment. It looks to a presence and perfection and purpose beyond all material form – to the reality of God, its true source and goal. This is where the real break with old fashioned materialism comes. For the old-fashioned materialist, the final reality is 'matter' – that is, a collection of particles, possessing the properties of position, velocity, mass, gravitational, electromagnetic and nuclear force, but having no purpose, value, awareness or responsibility. In such a world, the soul, as a continuous subject of uniquely apprehended experiences and responsible, creative freedom, is an anomaly or illusion. The self or subjectively conceived 'I' is constructed, perhaps, at the behest of society; it is a set of psychic by-products of physical processes in the brain. But there is no place in the materialist world-view for a free, moral, spiritual subject, whose proper destiny is to pursue moral excellence and realize unity with God. We must instead see the brain as a cybernetic system that can be programmed or electronically controlled, or even replaced by more efficient, inorganic thinking machines. All sense of the reality and importance of subjectivity disappears. Moreover, human behaviour will be modified most effectively by neurological engineering. This can replace the less effective idea of 'responsibility', which was a very inefficient conditioning mechanism to make people behave in socially desirable ways.

From a religious point of view, it can be pointed out that it is a denial of the obvious facts of subjectivity and freedom in the name of a very abstract theory for which there is no positive evidence and which there is great difficulty in even formulating coherently. That is not to say it is false; just to point out that it is far from being an obvious truth as it is sometimes taken to be. It is a highly disputable, poorly evidenced and very vaguely stated metaphysical theory.

For theistic believers the most basic reality is spiritual – the only self-sustaining being is God, who is personal, purposive, supremely worthwhile and aware. Believers do not at all deny the reality of the material world, but they would stress its total dependence upon God for its existence; and would not see why the material world, which God has brought into being from nothing, should not develop non-mechanistic, purposive, holistic, emergent and non-law-like characteristics, if God so desires it. In fact, it looks as if those are just the characteristics matter has developed, in the existence of the higher animals, and especially in mankind. Thus the physical structure of the central nervous system and the brain causes the genesis of one continuous subject of experiences, which then interacts in responsible and purposive ways with its material environment, through its own material properties.

The proposal that the brain should be treated just like a computer, modified and tampered with according to someone else's desires, is not a conclusion from any truly scientific theory. It is a proposal to treat persons as objects, to be disposed of and manipulated at will. In other words, it is not a scientific theory, but a basic moral perversion. The interesting thing is that this perversion has to be dressed up as a scientific theory – as what Jacques Monod calls 'the principle of objectivity'.[5] Of course, Monod does not *wish* to create a morally perverse view, but such is the implication of what he says.

How we treat people does depend on how we see them; our actions will be shaped by our vision of how things are. So if we see human beings as collections of purposeless physical particles, we will begin treating them as if they were just more complicated rocks, without inherent dignity or value. Whereas if we see them as transcendent subjects with a unique experience and a responsible freedom, we will have to cherish that uniqueness and respect that freedom in our own actions.

Believers should not wish to deny that the soul *is* the embodied person we think and see and know in the world. But, in speaking of the soul, they wish to stress that the most important characteristic of the material world is its inherent tendency to realize purposes and values and achieve consciousness of them; it has been purposively created by God to do just that. And the soul, even in its true and full embodiment, finds its deepest fulfilment in seeking a growing union with the spiritual reality of God. God is the true end of the soul, and in this sense, its goal, its proper purpose and true nature, lies beyond the physical universe. That is a strong reason for thinking that the subject embodied in this world may properly find other forms of experience and action, in contexts lying beyond this universe, wherein its God-given goal may be realized, its experiences woven into a meaningful pattern and its responses brought to an appropriate consummation. The semitic faiths speak of the 'resurrection of the body'. By this they mean that the human person will have a fuller life beyond death in community with others and in fulfilment of its own true nature. The Indian faiths speak of 'rebirth'. By this they mean that each person will live after death, perhaps in this world or perhaps in other forms of embodiment, until it works out its destiny – its *karma* – and attains a supreme spiritual goal of knowledge, freedom and bliss. These views are not so different as is sometimes thought, for they both speak of a continued yet new embodiment of the present person, and of an ultimate destiny of freedom from sorrow, ignorance and selfishness. We need have no inkling of what this ultimate state may be. We need only see that this subject-soul finds its true purpose in union with a reality transcending the physical, so we have no reason to limit it to the present form of its embodiment, and some reason to hope that it may find an appropriate form of fulfilment when this physical body becomes a corpse.

Properly understood, then, the sciences of cybernetics and neurophysiology do not threaten the spirituality of the soul at all. On the contrary, it is only a clear grasp of that spirituality that can prevent such sciences being misused by morally perverse tyrannies. Of course the soul depends on the brain, but the brain is not a machine. And the soul need not always depend on the brain, any more than a man need always depend on the womb that supported his life before birth. The most basic dependence of the soul is upon God, and it is in becoming conscious of the reality of God and learning to love and obey God that the soul discovers what its true nature is. Belief in the dignity of the soul and in a supreme spiritual reality, which theists know as God, go together. And that is why belief in God or in the reality of a supreme spiritual goal is the essential basis of a genuine and rational respect for the dignity and sacredness of the rational soul and of human life.

8

REASON,
RELIGION AND SCIENCE

IN MODERN WESTERN SOCIETY, the theologian finds himself standing in a very uncomfortable place. The days when theology was the queen of the sciences have gone; the sciences are pursued in laboratories and technological institutes. Theology is widely seen to be a matter of word-splitting, a matter of mere opinion and rhetoric. It is now harder to say that the whole universe shows the designing hand of a perfectly rational God, and that theologians have responsibility for elucidating His design and purpose for the world. Natural scientists tell us how the world is. Theologians have been forced to renounce their grandiose claims, one by one. Now they live in the border-lands of half-belief. Their schemes no longer encompass the universe. They sketch out nice ways of life or possible points of view, options for living at the periphery of the real hard quest for truth.

An intellectual earthquake has passed over the landscape, and where the theologian once stood on a high vantage point, surveying the whole scene, now he finds himself in a small hollow, not seeing very far and inexorably sinking in marshy ground. What can we do, from our marshy hollow, but utter a despairing cry of loss and nostalgia for the old landscape? On the firm high ground, itself about to be convulsed, no one listens. The voices from the marsh are faltering and divided; the siren voices of science are stronger, calling all to follow on the clear, wide road to the sea. We cannot turn back, they say; we must go on, pursuing truth to the bitter end. The way back is superstition and confusion. So, even when the cliffs ahead come into view and the sea waves are hard breaking on the rocks below, there can be no question of return.

Is it only nostalgia for which the theologian stands? Can theology not still, or even especially now, extend a warning hand, point a new direction, itself point to firmer ground? The reason for thinking that it may is that there is still one basic value shared between science and theology; perhaps the last remaining, it still seems to exercise a fascination. It is the value of truth.

Natural science is committed to the rational pursuit of truth, and therefore to the basic assumption that the world is amenable to reason. We will not be wholly deluded or obstructed in our search for the structure of reality, if we use reason systematically and well. That is the most basic assumption of the scientific world-view: reality is fundamentally rational, elegant in its laws and simple in its structures, open to the use of human reason at every level.

It is possible to deny this. There are those who say that the scientific enterprise is simply a by-product of western culture, that its values are not universally compelling. Truth itself is relative, they say; and what we think to be true depends on our own culture. There is no final, objective, absolute truth. Some things are true for me and others for you – depending on the interests and desires of our cultures. Truth is agreement by convention; it is not some sort of matching to the real structure of things. So there is no one rational structure of reality, which an objective, dispassionate investigation can discover by patient searching and inventive theorizing.

Many influential philosophers, who have been influenced by pragmatism – the theory that something is true if it works – hold views rather like this. What is true is what our group agrees about; and there is nothing against which such a claim could be assessed. If such a view is taken, all is lost. All human activities and values are culture-relative, and there is no reason to adopt one picture of things rather than another, if we can manage it. We may adopt an absolutist morality or abandon morality altogether, and neither course will be more or less reasonable than the other. We may simply adopt a view of the world and try to persuade others to follow us, or force them to do so if we wish. Rational persuasion will have no point unless we get others to think that reasoning is a good thing.

If that happens, the theologian has nothing to say. He may cling on to his own favourite world-picture, but it will be one whose day is past, overtaken by the irreversible onward march of technological and social advance. The real roots of human belief will be elsewhere, in visceral processes whose destiny is a self-destruction that mere thought will be powerless to prevent.

But of course this very statement assumes that every world-picture is not equally rational. The world really will hasten to destruction; there is an advance in at least technical skill; we really do know more about the world now than we did in medieval times. We cannot escape, in consistent thought, the realization that the human mind can discover truth and grows in its appropriation of it over the centuries. But in that case, there are two things to hold on to, two vitally important things that cannot consistently be surrendered – reason and truth. The human being does possess a special dignity and function. It is the place where reason brings truth to light, where the world becomes aware of itself, as a sphere in which reason thrives and grows, and understands itself more fully by its own activity.

In this world, the theologian finds his voice again. For he knows, through his tradition, of the world as the product of reason, as the sphere of rational activity, as purposively destined to let reason grow, by responsible human activity. And despite all appearances, he knows that in such a world morality can never be wholly abandoned. For morality, at root, is human action on the basis of the responsible use of reason. This is not the pallid humanist idea of reason, chattering endlessly among

common-room coffee-cups, emptily echoing above deep irrational depths of mindless passion. Humanism is not wrong, but
it is rootless. There is no view of reality, no firm truth upon
which it can be based. It tells us to respect humanity, in
ourselves and others; to preserve the dignity of man. And yet, in
a low but audible whisper, it tells us that it really knows, as we
all do, that man has no dignity, in the perspective of eternity.
There is nothing special about humanity; it will not survive; it is
a chance product of random mutation. Our fondness for it is
little more than a sort of magnified partiality, beyond rational
justification. In the light of reality, it is not surprising that the
exhortations of humanism seem weak and watery, powerless to
move the passionate will, unable to provide any vision other
than that of more pleasure for everybody.

The reasonableness of being, of which the theologian still
speaks, is other than this. His faith in God testifies that reason,
purpose and value are built into the deep structure of the
universe itself. It is the elegant ordering of reason that causes
the stars to circle in their galaxies. The value of reason is found
precisely in the appreciation of this beauty of order and
pattern. For this view, reason is not merely instrumental, a
mechanism for finding pleasure more efficiently. It is itself the
chief end and goal, as it is the origin, of all things. It is the
active rational process of delighting in its own creative
ordering of things. Reason is creative and finds its due fulfilment in the endless generation of new forms of beauty and
pattern to be enjoyed. And reason is morally ordered; for it is
ordered towards truth, and thus against whatever conceals
truth or impedes the search for it – lying, lack of trust and co-
operation, concealment and repression of all sorts. Moreover,
reason is essentially communal and co-operative. It is opposed
to the merely idiosyncratic and arbitrary; the making of excep-
tions in one's own case; the blind brute rule of passion. The
discoveries of reason are built up by co-operation and passed
on through teaching and learning. Reason aims at what is
universal and impartial; it inherently tends to transcend limited
self-interest and xenophobic restrictiveness.

It is in this way that an understanding of reason and truth is the fundamental, universal and firm foundation of morality. The sorts of morality that fall before the critical examination of reason are non-rational, compulsive, repressive systems of rules, whose only basis is psychological, biological or social conditioning, and whose only justification is survival or pleasure – a shoddy and ultimately disillusioning aim of human endeavour. If a firmer foundation for morality is to be sought, it must be in an understanding of reason, not as a narrow, instrumental, calculating faculty, but as a creative, imaginative discoverer of truth and beauty. Human persons are in fact unique and distinctive precisely in their possession of such reason. They are rational beings, in the sense that they can, by co-operative and creative effort, come to appreciate the elegance and beauty of the world, its mathematical structures and its ordered integration; and they can find their truest happiness in such rational activity and appreciation.

Plato, in his dialogue, *Phaedo*, remarks that any morality founded on the pursuit of pleasure must be a sorry and unattractive thing, since it seems to reduce human life to the level of any animal, which is most contented when it chews grass, and has nothing better to look forward to. 'A system of morality which is based on relative emotional values is a mere illusion, a thoroughly vulgar conception which has nothing sound in it and nothing true.'[1] The main pursuit of human life is, he says, wisdom or truth. It is that pursuit which distinguishes us from other animals, raises our lives above the level of sensuous pleasure and gives us a distinctively intellectual goal. If you ask the question, 'Why be rational?' there is, in a sense, no answer to be given. It is tempting to say, 'Because it will get you more of what you want, or get it more efficiently'. But that begs the question. For you must first believe that it is rational to get more of what you want, and that you should do what is rational. Otherwise, you could just go on getting what you want from moment to moment, as desires arise and pass away in the mind. Reason requires us often to defer present pleasure for the sake of future good.

But to make that sacrifice, you must first believe you should follow the dictates of reason rather than of impulse. And then you may discover that reason has its own goals, different from those of mere pleasure. Those goals cannot be undermined, unless reason itself is undermined.

First, and most obviously, anything that impedes the development of reason or its proper pursuit, the search for truth, is wrong. So lying and lack of trust are ruled out; honesty and fidelity, in the sense of trustworthiness, are enshrined as moral goals; without them, the search for truth is maimed and misdirected. Then the increase of knowledge is clearly also good. This is not just knowledge in the sense of knowing more facts, but it is getting a greater acquaintance with and appreciation of things as they truly are – as Plato put it, the true natures of things. Where other persons are concerned, this will mean achieving a sensitivity to and sympathy with their feelings, aspirations and values; for without such sensitivity, we cannot be said to have a just perception of how they really are. Sympathy and attentive regard are basic virtues. And with them, benevolence, concern for the well-being of others, must follow – it is just not possible to understand and sympathize with the suffering of another without being committed to relieving that suffering in some appropriate way. When we see that reason is concerned with uncovering the truth about other persons and how they are, we see more clearly that it is not a purely intellectual thing at all. It requires the sort of attentive regard and the disposition to respond appropriately that may properly be called 'love'. Then, justice is love distributed among all those who should claim our regard. The claim of rationality already contains within itself the requirement of impartiality upon which considerations of justice are founded.

A true understanding of reason will see that it is not just a passive faculty, which registers what occurs as though upon a blank sheet of paper. It is an active, organizing, imaginative faculty, which constructs theories, connects and evaluates data in various patterns and sequences of importance and relevance, and makes judgements upon the coherence, adequacy and consistency of wide-ranging interpretations of the world. It is a positive, creative attempt to understand and attend to the truth that meets us from day to day, to delight in it or respond to it with informed concern. It is quite wrong to see reason as an amoral, non-evaluative faculty – as though a perfectly rational person could also be a totally immoral person.

Certainly, a person can be a highly efficient calculator, somebody who can see the most efficient means to some goal, and then pursue it ruthlessly. We might call such a person rational, much as we might call a thief courageous or a successful egoist wise. He has the techniques of reason without its substance or point; and this sense of reason is maimed and defective. For reason, understood in its deepest sense, is the love and pursuit of truth. It requires a full understanding of the natures of things, and such an understanding is bound to modify our goals and purposes. Reason calls not only for calculation, but also for insight and discernment, for judgement and appropriate response. When reason is seen in that light, morality has a firm foundation in the rational nature of the soul, and the proper excellence of the soul, which is the exploration of that rationality by each person in his unique situation. We will only see morality as important, as placing an irresistible demand upon us that is also a supremely attractive ideal, when we hold firm to the knowledge that the soul is a subject of rational and responsible consciousness. Each of us has the task, in our own quite unique lives, of understanding as widely and sensitively as possible, and responding to what we rationally perceive as fully and appropriately as possible. In doing that, we fulfil our true natures, as beings with the capacity for rational love.

A rational commitment to morality, therefore, depends upon a perception of human nature; upon a perception of the human soul, as a being with the capacity and the responsibility to grow in wisdom and love. That, in turn, depends on the world being such as to contain beings of unique subjectivity, rational purpose and moral freedom. These concepts do not

make sense, there is no place for them, in a consistent materialism. They only really make sense when we see the universe as
one in which subjectivity, reason, purpose and love (that is,
sensitive attention and appropriate response to that which truly
is) lie at its foundation. For it is in that context that we can see
the soul as a finite image of the only true reality, as made in the
image of God. If there is no such God as the foundation and
goal of being, then the soul becomes an inexplicable anomaly
in the universe, a cosmic freak with a grossly over-inflated
sense of its own importance. And once you start to think that,
any sense of the unique dignity and worth of human life is in
danger of collapsing. It is in this way that a sense of the true
uniqueness and dignity of the human soul, a commitment to
reason, reverence and love, and a belief in God as the creator
of the universe go naturally together.

Once again this may seem to exclude non-theistic religious
views like that of Buddhism; but it is not meant to do so.
Buddhists would not typically speak of the soul as made in the
image of God or as a continuous centre of rational thought and
experience. They see the human person as a bundle of
qualities, mental and physical, without any purposive creator.
Yet they are strongly committed to the objective existence of a
moral law, the law of *karma*, in the universe. And they are
committed to the existence of a reality beyond time and
suffering, the reality of *nirvana*, which is the goal of human
striving. They are also committed to compassion for all beings
as the key to the attainment of *nirvana*. Thus Buddhism is quite
as anti-materialistic as theism. While the Buddhist way of
understanding the universe is naturally rather different from
the theistic way, nevertheless both views are wholly opposed to
secular materialism. They give human dignity and morality a
central place in the universe by founding them on spiritual
realities beyond the purview of the natural sciences; so each, in
different ways, defend the uniqueness of the human person as a
fundamentally spiritual being (which is what I mean by the
existence of the soul) and affirm that self-knowledge and
knowledge of the true goal of human striving are the most

important of all forms of knowledge. Perhaps it will be in a converging unity of these great religious traditions that the decisive response to materialism will be found.

I have tried to trace some of the ways in which a sense of the uniqueness of the soul has been undermined in much modern thought. And I have suggested that the inevitable consequence of this process is that morality itself is undermined and left without convincing rational justification. When the destroyers of the soul have done their work, they usually turn back from the moral consequences of their theories, and end with a rather lame and totally unconvincing attempt to reinstate a modified version of traditional morality. We have seen this in Jacques Monod, in Erich Fromm and Karl Marx in slightly different ways. A particularly clear example can be found on the last page of Richard Dawkins' very entertaining book, *The Selfish Gene*. Having argued for 214 pages that human life is totally governed by the genes, 'unconscious, blind, replicators', he now says, in the last sentence or two, 'It is possible that yet another unique quality of man is a capacity for genuine disinterested, true altruism. I hope so, but I am not going to argue the case one way or the other. . .' This is suitably tentative; but his last sentence of all reads: 'We, alone on earth, can rebel against the tyranny of the selfish replicators.'[2] The questions this raises are obvious: how can rational, responsible, altruistic, purposive, conscious conduct be accounted for on such a materialist theory? Why should he *hope* that altruism is possible, unless he really does have a basic sense of moral obligation? And isn't it odd to see morality as a rebellion against our true natures, instead of as a fulfilment of their potentialities?

I think it is clear that what has happened, yet again, is that any basis for morality has been effectively undermined by showing the real basis of human behaviour in determination by the genes, the favoured bits of matter in this theory. But a gesture towards the dead morality has to be made, and so it is given a short bow of respect – which in no way alters the fact that it has been efficiently dispatched. If we really do see that reason, altruism and love are somehow distinctively human and morally obligatory, we need an account of human nature that will enshrine and protect these beliefs. We need to speak of the soul as well as of the genes, and not reduce one to the other.

But if we do that, we may find ourselves seeing the basic nature of things in a non-reductivist and non-materialist way. It will no longer be obvious that 'scientific objectivism' is true. Rather, the soul itself may provide a better clue to the nature of things. In its subjectivity and rationality and freedom we may see pointers to how things ultimately are. What has blocked perception at this point is often a caricature of what God is. The God perceived by Nietzsche was a tyrant whose presence made human freedom impossible, because He really determined everything. He was a capricious will who made rationality impossible, because He demanded blind faith without any evidence. He was an all-seeing oppressor, who made individuality and subjectivity impossible, because He always watched the innermost workings of the mind. There was no escape possible from this all-seeing capricious tyrant; so He had to die, to make human autonomy possible.

At this point, the believer in God should be happy to co-operate in the killing of such a God, or such a distorted image of God. But he should also be aware that religion tends to breed such images, if it is not kept under constant criticism and examination. The priests, the guardians of tradition, can become the instruments of repression, of censorship, of unthinking dogmatism and unreflective conformity. Where religion is powerful, it can indeed attempt to destroy the freedom to think, to reflect, to criticize – it can demand unthinking obedience to authority; it can seek to destroy individual creativity by constant scrutiny and control of thought and behaviour. Even worse, religion can breed hatred and intolerance, as I try to impose my alleged certainties upon others or regard them as less than human for disagreeing with me. All these things can and do happen; Christians, for example, cannot fail to note how Jesus's harshest words are reserved for those called by the general term 'scribes and pharisees', the guardians of the religious tradition of Israel. We must be careful to note, too, that this should never be seen as an attack on the Jews – of whom, of course, Jesus was one. It is an attack on all religious hypocrisy, Christian as well.

Nevertheless, religion does not become false because it is misused and perverted. The scribes and pharisees guarded a tradition that did truly contain the words of life. What is needed is to find the true God behind the distorted image. God is no tyrant; He leaves human beings free – too free, we might sometimes think, in view of the great suffering we cause to each other. He is not capricious, but constant and unswerving love. The faith He asks is not blind assent to dogma, but a life of trusting obedience. Because the whole of creation is founded on reason, because God gives us freedom, because He gives us, as rational souls, the capacity for personal relationship with Himself – because of these things, human reason and freedom and love have a fundamental and indestructible value.

It is not so much that we would have no value, as people, if there were no God. That sounds as if our value is somehow arbitrarily placed upon us by some alien being, as though it was a price set on us by God. But that is a misleading picture. For it is a true insight that human souls do have unique and indestructible worth; that we are bound to respect and love them. The question is, what this shows about the real nature of the world; and whether it is indeed an insight into truth, or just some arbitrary preference for people. If we come to see human beings as machines for genes or assemblies of macro-molecules, then it becomes virtually impossible to see human existence as uniquely valuable or moral ideals as absolutely commanding or the rational pursuit of truth as more than the illusion of determination by a set of rationalizations. Then, as Paul Halmos puts it, in *The Faith of the Counsellors*, 'The question is primarily not whether the mechanistic account of love is true, but how we shall continue our progress in love, and indeed survive, when everybody thinks it is true'.[3]

From the theologians' point of view, the scientistic attack upon the soul is, in its extreme forms, a final and brutal assault upon the value and ultimacy of the personal in the universe, upon the truth and commanding will of God, and therefore in the end upon humanity itself. We cannot separate our view of morality, its character and binding force, from our view of how the world is. That is why belief in God or in an ultimate spiritual reality of supreme value is the only firm and intelligible defence of the moral worth and uniqueness of humanity. For we do not want respect and love for persons to be an option, of which we may or may not take account. We believe it to be a universal and overriding obligation – one that applies to everyone without exception and must come before any other considerations whatsoever. The only way to make sense of such an obligation, that makes obligation more than a matter of preference or choice or inclination, is to recognize that obligations are promulgated by a wise, perfect and loving creator. For to acknowledge that such a being is supremely wise is to acknowledge that His commands are supremely rational. To see that He is perfect in power and knowledge is to regard Him with reverence and awe, to follow His guidance out of respect for His greatness. To believe that He is supremely loving, that He offers a relationship of love to us, is to respond to Him with glad and free obedience. And to understand that, as creator, He is the sole ultimate cause of our lives and all the good things we have, and that He is so by His own free choice, is to bind us in gratitude to Him. If such a being calls for our obedience to His command, there is the best possible reason for taking that command to be of absolutely overriding importance. Thus God does provide a wholly intelligible foundation for the absolute claims of morality, in a way that nothing else could.

But we can say more. It also helps to make talk of overriding claims intelligible if we can see that our response to them will make a real and important difference to the way the world is. We can see such a commitment as having a point, if it makes a distinctive contribution to the realization of some good purpose – not merely for the agent. Ideally, this contribution would not take the form simply of a means to an external end. The sort of person we choose to be would itself be part of the end. There would be, in other words, some sort of moral fulfilment; it would not be all self-sacrifice, without relation to the production of good. These beliefs, about the future realization of good and the inherent relation of personal sacrifice to that good, do imply certain causal beliefs about how the world will go and the place of moral commitment within that process. They make most sense when we think of a God who can both issue moral commands and also ensure, by His power, that there will be a future in which rational persons become what they have freely made themselves, by their moral responses. It is in this way that the existence of God makes sense of morality. It establishes absolute moral claims as universal, overriding and supremely rational. It makes morality the rational fulfilment of our natures, and not some arbitrary or pointless contradiction of our natural desires and inclinations. It makes human life something with a quite unique and distinctive character, purposively created to realize its own nature in freedom and by the response of love – the rational discernment of the claims of others upon us. Each human soul has a uniqueness, a capacity for free self-determination, a purpose and vocation that finds its greatest fulfilment in discovering an eternal relationship of love in which morality is transcended. It is transcended, not by being rejected, but by being transformed from a demand into a delight, from a hard discipleship into a supremely fulfilling devotion.

So the existence and importance of morality, the perception of the true nature of the soul as a unique and irreplaceable subject that transcends and yet is immanent in its material expressions, and the discernment of God as the ultimate and supremely transcendent Subject are tied together. Morality is the beginning of that union of the soul with God, which is completed in love. Love is essentially connected with understanding, with reason and truth, with attentive regard and sensitive judgement. Thus we cannot divorce our basic commitments from our perception of things. Religious faith is not some irrational leap beyond any evidence. It is a fundamental commitment to the rationality of being. It assures us that creative reason is at the origin and heart of things; that the exercise of it is our proper vocation; that its pursuit gives to human life a distinctive dignity and worth.

When the theologian speaks of reason, then, he speaks of the Divine Reason, the *Logos* of the universe, the wisdom and intelligibility of being. He is not speaking of what David Hume called 'the slave of the passions', the instrumental deviser of more effective means to obtaining ends set by non-rational desire. Reason, as seen by the theologian, is not a mechanism that happens to have been conducive to the survival of the human species. It is the very mind and heart, the inner pattern, of the universe and its creative source.

It is probable that the early Greek philosophers, who first began to explore the universe as the expression of *nous*, or mind, had too severely intellectual a notion of reason. It was that belief that led eventually to the rise of the natural sciences, as people came to feel that the world was ordered by one non-arbitrary being, striving to obtain the richest set of effects from the simplest set of basic principles. But with the Greek philosophers, science could not come to fruition, because they despised the flesh, the material world, as basically non-rational. Reason, for them, was an affair of the intellect, of pure thought. To achieve rationality, you had to leave the material world behind and discover the purely intellectual world of ideal concepts, the Platonic 'forms'.

It was Christian theology, with its fundamental idea of the incarnation of the *Logos* in matter itself, which was able to found the view that the material world itself was ordered on rational principles. Thus Isaac Newton set himself to read the 'book of nature' that the Divine Mind had written. Theoretical science was able to begin, because of the faith that uncreated reason had written the rules that created reason could now decipher. It took a long time for Christian thought to free itself from the anti-experimental mentality of Greek philosophy. But the seeds of such a breakaway were sown as soon as it was said that the Divine Reason had been supremely expressed in a particular historical place and time – so that it could only be discerned by factual investigation, not by pure theory.

Not only is there an inner connection between morality and belief in God, as the source of its objectivity and authority; there is also an inner connection between science and belief in God. For science has a fundamental faith, a faith in the rationality of the world, and in the capacity of human reason to discover the truth about the world by a combination of disciplined attention and thought. But if this is true, how has it come about that, since the Enlightenment and the rise of the scientific world-view in the seventeenth and eighteenth centuries, science and religion have so often been seen in opposition? How can that resolute pursuit of truth, which has marked the natural sciences, have led to the apparent rejection of purpose in the world, of objective value and of God?

The reason is partly because of those battles about evolution and astronomy that resulted from a misplaced dogmatism on the part of some religious believers, from a sort of theological imperialism that would not allow the natural sciences authority in their proper sphere. But more deeply it was the growth of a general theory of mechanist materialism, a view that the world was a closed and complete system of purely mechanical causes, which disallowed any supernatural 'interventions'. This was, of course, a misplaced dogmatism on the part of some scientific theorists, a sort of scientistic imperialism that left no place for religion at all. It was, from the first, an over-general extrapolation from a range of particular scientific disciplines. It was a restriction and limitation of the goals and methods of reason, which has reduced the world to an abstract and skeletal reconstruction, a shadow of a reality hardly recognizable as the one in which we live and breathe.

The so-called 'scientific world-view' arises from a one-sided vision of the nature of things. Just as the Greeks tended to underplay the value of the material, so the scientific mechanists have underplayed the value of the personal. They attempt to apply to the whole of reality techniques that have high explanatory value for more precise, verifiable and quantifiable phenomena in artificially controlled situations. What is needed is to recover the sense of reason as a form of just discernment of the world in its comprehensive totality, in its uniqueness, originality, purposiveness and privacy, as well as in its regularity, predictability, mechanism and public measurability. We need to recognize that the sciences are essentially evaluative, in their commitment to truth and objectivity, and that here they overlap with morality and with faith (understood as commitment to a transcending value).

There is a battle joined in our culture between an aggressive scientism, which seeks to persuade us, on alleged scientific evidence, that talk of God, the soul and morality is finished, and the defence of those values that are essential to a truly human existence. It is a battle for the soul, and the scientistic attacks on human uniqueness, conscience and the sense of duty have led to assaults on freedom and truth itself. It is at this point, however, that the attackers begin to destroy themselves. For in undermining the values of truth and freedom, they undermine the very values upon which they are based. They see human life as without purpose, value or meaning. But, in doing so, they appeal to the very values of truth, self-knowledge and courage they already claim to have undermined. Thus they express the integrity and intrinsic dignity of human existence, even as they explicitly disclaim it. Their case is built upon a contradiction and cannot prevail.

There is little that is more important in our culture than to reaffirm the existence of the soul and to show the shallowness of views denying it. For the most important thing in life, in the end, is to discover what we truly are and to live accordingly. If we are souls, created by God to know and love Him for ever, nothing could be more important for us to realize than that. The battle for the soul is real. What is at stake is human freedom and dignity, morality and truth, the survival of human beings as moral and responsible beings. I have tried to show that, in the end, commitment to these things depends upon realizing that reality is fundamentally spiritual in nature, that it is founded on and directed by reason, purpose and subjectivity. But the crucial battleground is the nature of humanity. And the battle is about whether human personhood is a random product of material, unconscious forces, or the presence of transcendent subjectivity in the material world.

In a world in which broad theoretical decisions are complex and difficult, the issue may seem finely balanced; the weight of science may seem to incline the scales towards the materialistic view. But in our own self-consciousness, our awareness of our thoughts and feelings, in our awareness of moral responsibility, our rational reflection and our sense of God, of a spiritual realm or at the least of a 'need to rebel' against the merely material, we find ourselves committed in practice to the assertion of our transcendence over nature and its laws.

Then, when we consider more carefully the nature of the sciences, and we perceive their limits, their restriction to the general, the objective, the measurable and the repeatable, we may see that they seem to incline to materialism only because they confine themselves to certain aspects of the material. And when we consider the faith-commitment of the sciences to reason and truth, to the search for elegance and beauty, for rational understanding and just perception, then we may see that they, too, point to a spiritual basis for the world. So we may begin to discern the dawning of a new age, in which science, morality and religion will no longer clash one with the other. Rather, they may seek to achieve an integrated vision of things, which will bring us a clearer vision of the wholeness of creation.

To show this in detail and with full conviction is a task for a person who has full command of scientific knowledge in many fields; who has a deep understanding of human experience and creativity; who has a broad sensitivity to the religious and moral traditions of mankind and a keen grasp of the techniques of philosophical argumentation. But, in the absence of such a one, it may take a theologian to formulate, stumblingly, a vision he feels to be forming on the edge of consciousness, the recovery of an integrated vision of existence; to sketch its outlines even if he cannot master the intricate details of its structure. Such a theologian will be a fool speaking to the wise, claiming to remind them of what they have forgotten and of what they stand to lose. He will say that morality is not a rebellion against truth; that truth is not a rebellion against God; that God is not the great subverter of the soul. He will not make any claim to see the truth more clearly, from some remote, superior vantage point. But he will place his flag upon the human soul, the soul that God has made and claimed for his own by incarnation and passion, and say that this is not negotiable ground. Iconoclasm has performed its necessary task. Now the ground is cleared. It is time to stand firm, ready to build anew.

NOTES

Chapter 1

1. F. Nietzsche, *Die fröhliche Wissenschaft* 3, 108 (1882).
2. F. Nietzsche, *Thus Spake Zarathustra* (1884), Prologue; trans. T. Commone (Allen and Unwin, 1923).
3. Voltaire, *Epitres xcvi: A l 'Auteur du Livre des Trois Imposteurs* (1858).
4. Cf. P. Nowell-Smith, *Ethics* (Penguin, 1954), ch. 3 and Richard Robinson, *An Atheist's Values* (OUP, 1964).
5. Mark 8:34; Matthew 25:40; 6:19–24.
6. Mark 9:43; Matthew 25:1–12; Matthew 22:13.
7. Mark 12:28–31.
8. J-P. Sartre, *Being and Nothingness*, trans. H. Barnes (Methuen, 1969), p. 625ff.
9. In an interview in 1964, recalled by John Bowker in *Making Moral Decisions* (SPCK, 1969), p. 55.
10. Proverbs 29:18.

Chapter 2

1. I. Kant, *General History of Nature and Theory of the Heavens* (1755), trans. W. D. Hastie, as *Kant's Cosmogony* (Maclehose, Glasgow, 1900).
2. C. Darwin, *The Origin of Species* (1859).
3. Aquinas, *Summa Theologiae* (Blackfriars ed. 1964), Qu. 76, Art. I.
4. Ibid., Qu. 118, 2 ad. 2.
5. For interesting, accurate accounts, cf. Paul Davies, *God and the New Physics* (Dent, 1983); John Polkinghorne, *The Particle Play* (W. H. Freeman, 1979); Fritjof Capra, *The Tao of Physics* (Fontana, 1976).
6. T. Dobzhansky, *The Biology of Ultimate Concern* (New American Library, 67), p. 125.
7. Rupert Sheldrake, *The New Science of Life* (Paladin/Granada, 1983).
8. P. S. Laplace, *Essai philosophique sur les probabilités* (Batchelier, Paris, 1825), p. 3.
9. Cf. note 5, above. Also, a fascinating book by D. J. Bartholomew, *God of Chance* (SCM Press, 1984).

10. Cf. the view of a leading quantum physicist, E. Wigner, 'Remarks on the mind–body question', in *The Scientist Speculates*, ed. I. J. Good (Heinemann, 1962).

11. Richard Taylor, *Action and Purpose* (Englewood Cliffs, NY, 1966), argues that purposive causality is not reducible to mechanistic causality.

12. Jacques Monod, *Chance and Necessity* (Collins, 1972), p. 30.

13. Ibid., p. 110.

14. Ibid., p. 31.

15. Ibid., p. 158.

16. Ibid., p. 161. Three books by respected biologists that take views sympathetic to those of this chapter are: A. R. Peacocke, *Creation and the World of Science* (Clarendon, 1979); Sir Alister Hardy, *The Living Stream* (Collins, 1965); M. Polanyi, *The Tacit Dimension* (Routledge, Kegan Paul, 1967).

Chapter 3

1. Desmond Morris, *The Naked Ape* (Jonathan Cape, 1967), p. 156.

2. Ibid., p. 158.

3. Ibid., p. 157.

4. Konrad Lorenz, *On Aggression* (Methuen, 1966).

5. Ibid., p. 69.

6. Ibid., p. 70.

7. Ibid., p. 71.

8. E. O. Wilson, *Sociobiology* (Harvard University Press, 1975), p. 3.

9. Ibid., p. 120.

10. Ibid., p. 4.

11. E. O. Wilson, *On Human Nature* (Harvard University Press, 1978), p. 3.

12. A. Einstein, quoted in F. Capra, *The Tao of Physics* (Fontana, 1976), p. 49.

13. Niels Bohr, *Atomic Physics and the Description of Nature* (CUP, 1934), p. 57.

14. E. O. Wilson, *Sociobiology* (Harvard University Press), p. 129.

15. Ibid., p. 562.

16. Ibid., p. 575.

17. B. F. Skinner, *Beyond Freedom and Dignity* (Penguin, 1973), p. 193.

18. C. H. Waddington, *The Ethical Animal* (Allen and Unwin, 1960).

19. T. H. Huxley, *Evolution and Ethics* (Pilot Press, London, 1947).

20. Herbert Spencer, *Principles of Sociology* (1897).

Chapter 4

1. S. Freud, *The Ego and the Id* (Hogarth Press, 1962), p. 47.

2. Ibid., p. 84.

3. E. Fromm, *Man For Himself* (Routledge, Kegan Paul, 1949), p. 225.

4. Aristotle, *Nichomachean Ethics*, I. Good general books on the subject of this chapter are: J. C. Flugel, *Man, Morals and Society* (Duckworth, 1945); Freud, *Moses and Monotheism*, trans. K. Jones (Hogarth Press, 1957); Freud, *Totem and Taboo*, trans. J. Strachey (Routledge, Kegan Paul, 1950); Freud, *The Future of an Illusion*, trans. Scott (Hogarth Press, 1962); Freud, *New Introductory Lectures on Psycho-analysis*, trans. J. Strachey (Penguin, 1973).

NOTES

Chapter 5

1. Marx and Engels, 'Manifesto of the Communist Party', in *The Essential Left* (Allen and Unwin, 1960), p. 12.
2. Ibid., p. 31.
3. Ibid., p. 25.
4. Ibid., p. 33.
5. Bottomore and Rubel, *Marx: Selected Writings in Sociology and Social Philosophy* (Penguin, 1970); and *Marx, Early Texts*, ed. D. McLellan (Blackwell, 1971).
6. Cf. Amos 5:7–24.
7. Ruth Benedict, *Patterns of Culture* (Routledge, Kegan Paul, 1968), p. 199.
8. Marx, *Selected Writings. . .* , p. 83.
9. *Communist Manifesto*, p. 33.
10. Ashley Montagu, *Anthropology and Human Nature* (P. Sargent, 1982).
11. Talcott Parsons, *Essays in Sociological Theory* (Free Press, 1964).
12. Ruth Benedict, *Patterns of Culture* (Routledge, Kegan Paul, 1968).
13. Ibid., p. 201.
14. H. L. A. Hart, *The Concept of Law* (Oxford University Press, 1976).

Chapter 6

1. Augustine, 'Of the Morals of the Catholic Church', ch. 15 in *A Select Library of the Nicene and Post-Nicene Fathers*, ed. P. Schaff (Christian Publishing Co., New York, 1886–90), vol. 4.
2. P. T. Geach, *God and the Soul* (Routledge, Kegan Paul, 1969), p.122.
3. P. T. Geach, *The Virtues* (Cambridge University Press, 1977), p.9.
4. John Austin, *The Province of Jurisprudence Determined*, ed. H. L. A. Hart, 1954.
5. P. Foot, *Virtues and Vices* (Basil Blackwell, 1978), p.156.
6. R. M. Hare, *Moral Thinking* (Clarendon Press, Oxford, 1981).
7. John Rawls, *A Theory of Justice* (Oxford University Press, 1973).
8. Francis Crick, *Of Molecules and Men* (University of Washington Press, 1968).

Chapter 7

1. Julian Huxley, *Man and his Future*, ed. G. Wolstenholme (Churchill Press, 1963), p. 17.
2. B. A. Farrell, 'On the Design of a Conscious Device', in *Mind*, July 1970.
3. Aquinas, *Summa Theologiae*, Ia, 75, 6.
4. Genesis 2:7.
5. Jacques Monod, *Chance and Necessity* (Collins, 1972), p. 30.

Chapter 8

1. Plato, *Phaedo*, 68C.
2. Richard Dawkins, *The Selfish Gene* (Oxford University Press, 1976), p. 215.
3. Paul Halmos, *The Faith of the Counsellors* (Constable, 1977), p. 200.

INDEX

INDEX